CAREERS FOR

# LEGAL EAGLES

### & Other Law-and-Order Types

Careers for You Series

# CAREERS FOR

# LEGAL
# EAGLES

## & Other Law-and-Order Types

## BLYTHE CAMENSON

### SECOND EDITION

### McGraw·Hill

New York   Chicago   San Francisco   Lisbon   London   Madrid   Mexico City
Milan   New Delhi   San Juan   Seoul   Singapore   Sydney   Toronto

The *McGraw·Hill* Companies

**Library of Congress Cataloging-in-Publication Data**

Camenson, Blythe
  Careers for legal eagles & other law-and-order types / Blythe Camenson—
2nd ed.
    p.  cm.  —  (McGraw-Hill careers for you series)
    ISBN 0-07-143858-0  (alk. paper)
    1.  Law—Vocational guidance—United States.    I.  Title: Careers for legal
eagles and other law-and-order types.    II.  Title.    III.  Series.

  KF297.Z9C358    2005
  340′.023′73—dc22                                                              2004018877

1 2 3 4 5 6 7 8 9 0    DOC/DOC    0 9 8 7 6 5

ISBN 0-07-143858-0

McGraw-Hill books are available at special quantity discounts to use as premiums and
sales promotions, or for use in corporate training programs. For more information,
please write to the Director of Special Sales, Professional Publishing, McGraw-Hill,
Two Penn Plaza, New York, NY 10121-2298. Or contact your local bookstore.

This book is printed on acid-free paper.

*To Sara Goodman, my friend
and favorite legal eagle*

# Contents

# Acknowledgments

The author would like to thank the following legal eagles for providing information about their careers:

| | |
|---|---|
| Barbara F. Arrants | Public Defender |
| Dan P. Clark | Court Reporter |
| Kimberly Diehl | Jailer |
| Mike W. Elliott | Assistant District Attorney |
| Gist Fleshman | Clerk of the Court |
| Jennifer Franks | Legal Secretary |
| Chris Goodwin | Investigator |
| M. J. Goodwin | Family Law |
| Barbara Grace Lake | Legal Assistant |
| James Lanuti | Circuit Court Judge |
| Bob Lemons | Arson Investigator |
| Joe Nickell | Undercover Investigator |
| Ramesh Nyberg | Homicide Detective |
| Kent Reeves | Bailiff |
| Timothy T. Speed Jr. | Security Supervisor |
| Gigi Starnes | Legal Secretary |
| John Wiorek | Research Attorney |

The editors would like to thank Josephine Scanlon for preparing this second edition.

# CHAPTER ONE

# Options for Legal Eagles

rime doesn't pay, they say, but that expression is aimed at criminals. A vast array of careers for law-abiding and justice-seeking individuals exists on the right side of the law—and they all offer legitimate paychecks.

But there's no room for armchair legal eagles here. The careers covered in this book put you out where the action is. Some of the work is detail oriented, some is frustrating, and some involves danger—but there's no greater reward than tracking down real criminals, prosecuting them, and seeing justice at work.

The people who work in law careers give of themselves in many different capacities, providing valuable service to their communities and to the nation.

## Jobs for Legal Eagles

You might be concerned that the only route to a career in law is the long haul—years and years of law school, bar exams, and stiff competition for jobs with the best firms. That is true for most attorneys.

But there are many other paths that can lead you to an exciting law-related career. Take a look at the following overview of career areas from which you can choose, then read on to see what they involve.

## Attorneys at Law

Sometimes it seems that the number of lawyers with whom we are readily familiar is countless. Some are involved in high-profile cases that attract public interest; others become known for handling specific types of cases in large cities. In addition, TV shows, movies, and novels set in the legal arena have introduced a variety of fictional attorneys who are often as well known as their real-life counterparts.

In any of these situations, lawyers either defend or prosecute a defendant. Criminal lawyers operate their own practices, work for private law firms, or represent clients under the auspices of the public defender's office. Lawyers who work for state attorneys general, prosecutors, and courts play a key role in the criminal justice system. At the federal level, attorneys investigate cases for the Department of Justice or other agencies. Also, lawyers at every government level help develop programs, draft laws, interpret legislation, establish enforcement procedures, and argue civil and criminal cases on behalf of the government.

But criminal trial work is not the only option open to lawyers. Just as doctors can gear their careers toward a particular specialty, so can lawyers. Chapter 2 will introduce you to a variety of law specializations.

## Judges

Judges apply the law. They oversee the legal process that, in courts of law, resolves civil disputes and determines guilt in criminal cases according to federal and state laws and the laws of local jurisdictions.

Judges preside over cases touching on virtually every aspect of society, from traffic offenses to disputes over management of professional sports, from the rights of huge corporations to the question of disconnecting life support equipment for a terminally ill patient. Judges must ensure that trials and hearings are conducted fairly and that the court administers justice in a manner that safeguards the legal rights of all parties involved.

Although not all judges have been lawyers first, most have completed law school and have worked as practicing attorneys. Chapter 3 will introduce you to this demanding career.

## Court Staff

Most of us are familiar with the different personnel who work in courtrooms, thanks to Court TV and high-profile cases that are staples of television news. You've seen the judge and the bailiff and the court reporter. But there are others who work behind the scenes—in jobs that might be just right for you. See Chapter 4 for an inside look at courtroom life.

## Paralegals

Not all legal work requires a law degree. Lawyers are often aided in their work by paralegals, who are also known as legal assistants. Paralegals perform many of the same tasks as lawyers, except for those tasks considered to be the practice of law.

Paralegals can enter this exciting field through a formal training program or, sometimes, be trained on the job. In Chapter 5 you'll meet an experienced paralegal who has a lot to say about this particular career path.

## Legal Secretaries

Most organizations employ secretaries to perform and coordinate office activities and to ensure that information gets disseminated in a timely fashion to staff and clients. In law-related enterprises, lawyers, judges, managers, paralegals, and other support staff rely on legal secretaries to keep administrative operations under control. The specific duties of legal secretaries depend upon their level of responsibility and the type of firm in which they work. See Chapter 6 for more information on this field.

## Law Enforcement Officers

The safety of our nation's cities, towns, and highways greatly depends on the work of police officers, deputy sheriffs, detectives, and special agents whose responsibilities range from controlling traffic to preventing and investigating crimes. In Chapter 7 you will learn all about the various paths open to you in the field of law enforcement.

## Investigators

Fancy yourself a Magnum, P.I., type, or maybe another Kinsey Millhone, Sue Grafton's star detective? The field of private investigation can be exciting and glamorous; it can also be tedious and dull. For every undercover operation, there are hundreds of hours spent on the telephone or surfing the Net, and an equal number sitting in a car at a stakeout, cupping a mug of cold coffee. Chapter 8 will give you an inside look at what it's really like to work in private investigation.

## Correctional Officers

Correctional officers are charged with protecting the security and safety of persons who have been arrested, who are awaiting trials or other hearings, or who have been convicted and sentenced to serve time in a correctional institution. You have probably never been in a jail or prison. Do the movies portray life there accurately? You'll meet a real-life prison guard in Chapter 9—she'll fill you in.

## Security Guards

Security guards work in a variety of settings, and often the work is routine, even dull. But every once in a while, a security guard remembers why he or she was hired—and why it pays to be prepared for the occasions when something does go wrong. Learn more about this field from a security guard in Chapter 10.

## Choosing Your Field

If you're reading this book, chances are you're already considering a career in one of the many areas of the wide-open field of law. But perhaps you're not sure of the working conditions the different fields offer or which area best suits your personality, skills, and lifestyle.

There are several factors to consider when deciding which path to follow. Each field demands different levels of responsibility and commitment. To identify which occupations match your expectations, you need to know what each job entails.

Ask yourself the following questions. Then, as you go through this book, compare your responses to the information provided by the professionals interviewed in the following chapters. Their comments will help you pinpoint which fields most interest you and eliminate those that would clearly be the wrong choice.

- How much time are you willing to commit to training? Some skills can be learned on the job or in a year or two of formal training; others can take considerably longer.
- Do you want to work in an office behind a desk, or would you prefer to be out and about, patrolling a beat or meeting with clients in their homes—or in prison?
- Can you handle a certain amount of stress on the job, or would you prefer a quiet—and safe—environment?
- How much money do you expect to earn starting out and after you have a few years of experience under your belt? Salaries and earnings vary greatly for each profession, so it's important to match your expectations with the right career path.
- How much independence do you require? Do you want to be your own boss, or will you be content as a salaried employee?

- Would you rather work daytime hours, or would you prefer evenings and weekends?
- Can you pay attention to detail and handle paperwork, legal documents, and reports?

Knowing what your expectations are, then comparing them to the realities of the work, will help you make informed choices.

## The Training You'll Need

The training required for law-related careers varies greatly. Some positions are entry-level, requiring no more than a high school education. Some demand that you be physically fit and have some prior work experience. Others require specific skills and education, from a technical training program to two or four years of college. Still others require several years of postgraduate study.

## For More Information

In the Appendix you will find professional associations for many of the career paths explored in this book. Most have websites that offer extensive information, and many provide links to other helpful resources.

# CHAPTER TWO

# Attorneys at Law

ociety is smitten with attorneys. Novels featuring lawyers are staples of the bestseller lists, and most major movie stars have played attorneys at some point in their careers. Television programs might include more attorneys than members of any other profession, whether it's one of the "Law and Order" series or an actual trial on Court TV.

The more detailed aspects of the job depend upon a lawyer's field of specialization and position. Although all lawyers are licensed to represent parties in court, some appear in court more frequently than others. Trial lawyers, who specialize in trial work, must be able to think quickly and speak with ease and authority. In addition, familiarity with courtroom rules and strategy is particularly important in trial work. Still, trial lawyers spend the majority of their time outside the courtroom, conducting research, interviewing clients and witnesses, and handling other details in preparation for trial.

Lawyers can work for large or small firms, operate their own private practices, or represent clients as public defenders. They work in either criminal or civil law or both.

## Professional Opportunities

Once you're sworn in as a lawyer, there are many different career paths within the profession open to you. The job duties vary greatly, as you'll discover from the following descriptions.

## Criminal Law

In criminal law, attorneys represent individuals charged with crimes and argue their cases in courts of law. These lawyers may work in private practice, as part of a legal firm, or for the public defender's office.

## Civil Law

In civil law, attorneys assist clients with litigation, wills, trusts, contracts, mortgages, titles, and leases. Some manage a person's property as trustee or, as executor, see that provisions of a client's will are carried out. Others handle only public-interest cases, civil or criminal, that have a potential impact extending well beyond the individual client.

Other lawyers work for legal-aid societies—private, nonprofit organizations established to serve disadvantaged people. These lawyers generally handle civil rather than criminal cases.

## Specializations

Aside from criminal law, lawyers may specialize in a number of areas. Some specializations with civil law include:

- bankruptcy
- environmental law
- family law
- insurance law
- intellectual property law
- international law
- probate
- public defense
- real estate law

## House Counsel

Lawyers are sometimes employed full-time by a single client. If the client is a corporation, the lawyer is known as house counsel and usually advises the company concerning legal issues related to its business activities. These issues might involve patents, government regulations, contracts with other companies, property interests, or collective-bargaining agreements with unions.

## Government Attorneys

A significant number of attorneys are employed at the various levels of government. Lawyers who work for state attorneys general, prosecutors, public defenders, and courts play a key role in the criminal justice system. At the federal level, attorneys investigate cases for the U.S. Department of Justice and other agencies. Government lawyers also help develop programs, draft and interpret laws and legislation, establish enforcement procedures, and argue civil and criminal cases on behalf of the government.

## Law Clerks

Law clerks are fully trained attorneys who choose to work with a judge, either for a one- to two-year stint out of law school to gain experience before practicing law or as a full-time professional career. Their duties involve mainly research and writing reports.

## Law Professors

A relatively small number of trained attorneys work in law schools. Most are faculty members who specialize in one or more subjects, and others serve as administrators. Some work full-time in nonacademic settings and teach part-time.

# Working Conditions

Lawyers do most of their work in offices, law libraries, and courtrooms. They sometimes meet in clients' homes or places of business and, when necessary, in hospitals or prisons. They may travel to attend meetings, gather evidence, and appear before courts, legislative bodies, and other authorities.

Salaried lawyers usually have structured work schedules. Lawyers who are in private practice may work irregular hours while conducting research, conferring with clients, or preparing briefs during nonoffice hours.

Lawyers often work long hours, and of those who regularly work full-time, about half work fifty hours or more per week. At times, they face particularly heavy pressure, especially when a case is being tried.

Although legal work generally is not seasonal, the work of tax lawyers and other specialists may be an exception. Because lawyers in private practice often determine their own workloads and the point at which they will retire, many stay in practice well beyond the usual retirement age.

No matter the setting, whether acting as advocate or prosecutor, all attorneys interpret the law and apply it to specific situations. This requires excellent research and communication abilities. Preparation for court includes keeping abreast of the latest laws and judicial decisions.

Lawyers perform in-depth research into the purposes behind applicable laws and into judicial decisions that have been applied to those laws under circumstances similar to those currently faced by the client. Lawyers are increasingly using technology to perform their varied tasks more efficiently.

While all lawyers continue to use law libraries to prepare cases, some supplement their search of conventional printed sources with computer sources, such as the Internet and legal databases. Software is used to search the legal literature automatically and to identify legal texts relevant to a specific case. In litigation involving many supporting documents, lawyers may use computers to organize and index material. Lawyers also utilize electronic filing, videoconferencing, and voice-recognition technology to share information more effectively with other parties involved in a case.

# Training for Attorneys

To practice law in the courts of any state or other jurisdiction, a person must be licensed by that jurisdiction, or admitted to its bar, under rules established by the jurisdiction's highest court. All states require that applicants for admission to the bar pass a written bar examination; most jurisdictions also require applicants to pass a separate written ethics examination. Lawyers who have been admitted to the bar in one jurisdiction occasionally may be admitted to the bar in another without taking an examination if they meet the latter jurisdiction's standards of good moral character and have a specified period of legal experience. Federal courts and agencies set their own qualifications for those practicing before or in them.

To qualify for the bar examination in most states, an applicant usually must earn a college degree and graduate from a law school accredited by the American Bar Association (ABA) or the proper state authorities. ABA accreditation signifies that the law school, particularly its library and faculty, meets certain standards developed to promote quality legal education. The ABA currently accredits 188 law schools; others are approved by state authorities only.

With certain exceptions, graduates of schools not approved by the ABA are restricted to taking the bar examination and practicing in the state or other jurisdiction in which their school is located; most of these schools are in California.

In 2002, eight states accepted the study of law in a law office as qualification for taking the bar examination; three jurisdictions—California, the District of Columbia, and New Mexico—now accept the study of law by correspondence. Several states require registration and approval of students by the state's board of law examiners, either before the students enter law school or during their early years of legal study.

Although there is no nationwide bar examination, forty-eight states, the District of Columbia, Guam, the Northern Mariana Islands, Puerto Rico, and the Virgin Islands require the six-hour Multistate Bar Examination (MBE) as part of the overall bar examination; the MBE is not required in Louisiana and Washington. The MBE covers issues of broad interest, and sometimes a locally prepared state bar examination is given in addition to the MBE. The three-hour Multistate Essay Examination (MEE) is used as part of the bar examination in several states. States vary in their use of MBE and MEE scores.

Many states have begun to require Multistate Performance Testing (MPT) to test the practical skills of beginning lawyers. This program has been well received, and many more states are expected to require performance testing in the future. Requirements vary by state, although the test usually is taken at the same time as the bar exam and is a one-time requirement.

The required college and law school education usually takes seven years of full-time study after high school—four years of undergraduate study, followed by three years of law school. Law school applicants must have a bachelor's degree to qualify for admission. To meet the needs of students who can attend only part-time, a number of law schools have night or part-time divisions, which usually require four years of study; about one in ten graduates from ABA-approved schools attended part-time.

Although there is no recommended "prelaw" major, prospective lawyers should develop proficiency in writing and speaking, reading, researching, analyzing, and thinking logically—skills needed to succeed both in law school and in the profession. Regardless of major, a multidisciplinary background is recommended. Courses in English, foreign languages, public speaking, government, philosophy, history, economics, mathematics, and computer science, among others, are useful. Students interested in a particular aspect of law may find related courses helpful. For example, prospective patent lawyers need to gain a strong background in engineering or science, and future tax lawyers must have extensive knowledge of accounting.

Acceptance by most law schools depends on the applicant's ability to demonstrate an aptitude for the study of law, usually through good undergraduate grades, the Law School Admission Test (LSAT), the quality of the applicant's undergraduate school, any prior work experience, and, sometimes, a personal interview. However, law schools vary in the weight they place on each of these and other factors.

All law schools approved by the ABA, except those in Puerto Rico, require applicants to take the LSAT. Nearly all law schools require applicants to have certified transcripts sent to the Law School Data Assembly Service, which then submits applicants' LSAT scores and their standardized records of college grades to the law schools of their choice. Both this service and the LSAT are administered by the Law School Admission Council. Competition for admission to many law schools, especially the most prestigious ones, generally is intense, with the number of applicants to most law schools greatly exceeding the number that can be admitted.

During the first year or year and a half of law school, students usually study core courses, such as constitutional law, contracts, property law, tort law, civil procedure, and legal writing. In the remaining time, they may elect specialized courses in fields such as tax, labor, or corporate law. Law students often acquire practical experience by participating in school-sponsored legal clinic activities; in the school's moot court competitions, in which students conduct appellate arguments; in practice trials under the supervision of experienced lawyers and judges; and through research and writing on legal issues for the school's law journal.

A number of law schools have clinical programs in which students gain legal experience through practice trials and projects under the supervision of practicing lawyers and law school faculty. Law school clinical programs might include work in legal-aid clinics, for example, or on the staff of legislative committees.

Part-time or summer clerkships in law firms, government agencies, and corporate legal departments also provide valuable experience. Such training can lead directly to a job after graduation and can help students decide what kind of practice best suits them. Clerkships may also be an important source of financial aid.

In 2001, law students in fifty-two jurisdictions were required to pass the Multistate Professional Responsibility Examination (MPRE), which tests their knowledge of the ABA codes on professional responsibility and judicial conduct. In some states, the MPRE may be taken during law school, usually after completing a course on legal ethics.

Law school graduates receive the degree of juris doctor (J.D.) as the first professional degree. Advanced law degrees may be desirable for those planning to specialize, research, or teach. Some law students pursue joint degree programs, which usually require an additional semester or year of study. Joint degree programs are offered in a number of areas, including law and business administration or public administration.

## Employment Figures

Lawyers held about 695,000 jobs in 2002. About three out of four lawyers practiced privately, either in law firms or in solo practices. Most of the remaining lawyers held positions in government and with corporations and nonprofit organizations.

For those working in government, the greatest number were employed at the local level. In the federal government, lawyers work for many different agencies, but are concentrated in the Departments of Justice, Treasury, and Defense.

For those working outside of government, lawyers are employed as house counsel by public utilities, banks, insurance companies, real-estate agencies, manufacturing firms, and other business firms and nonprofit organizations. Some salaried lawyers also have part-time independent practices; others work part-time as lawyers and full-time in another occupation.

. . . . . . . . . . . . . . . . . .

# Earnings

In 2002, the median annual earnings of all lawyers was $90,290. The middle half of the occupation earned between $61,060 and $136,810. The lowest paid 10 percent earned less than $44,490; at least 10 percent earned more than $145,600.

Median annual earnings in the industries employing the largest numbers of lawyers in 2002 were as follows:

| | |
|---|---|
| Management of companies and enterprises | $131,970 |
| Federal government | $98,790 |
| Legal services | $93,970 |
| Local government | $69,710 |
| State government | $67,910 |

Salaries of experienced attorneys vary widely according to the employer's type, size, and location. Lawyers who own their own practices usually earn less than do those who are partners in law firms. When starting a new practice, lawyers may need to work part-time in other occupations to supplement their income until the practice is well established.

Most salaried lawyers are provided health and life insurance and contributions to retirement plans. Lawyers who practice independently are covered only if they arrange and pay for such benefits themselves.

# Practicing Law in Canada

In Canada, the legal profession is a self-governing body, regulated in each province by the regional Law Society. The Law Society determines whether an applicant can be licensed to practice law. The basic procedure for a prospective lawyer is to graduate from an approved law school and then complete the bar admission course in the province in which he or she wants to practice.

The academic prerequisite for taking the bar admission course is either graduation from a common law program approved by the Law Society in a Canadian university or acquisition of a certificate of qualification issued by the National Committee on Accreditation. There are sixteen universities in Canada that offer law courses approved by the Law Society. A student must meet the requirements of the university in order to study law. An approved law course takes three years to complete and leads to a bachelor of laws (LL.B.) or doctor of jurisprudence (J.D.) degree.

The specific requirements for the bar admission course differ among the provinces, but in general, the course is comprised of three phases: a skills phase, a substantive/procedural phase, and an articling phase. The skills and substantive/procedural phases usually run from eight to ten weeks each. The articling phase (the development of practical legal skills under the supervision of a lawyer) can last ten to twelve months. The bar examination is then taken upon successful completion of the bar admission course. All lawyers must join the Law Society in the province where they practice.

# What It's Really Like

## Barbara F. Arrants, Public Defender

Barbara Arrants earned her B.S. in psychology in 1985 from the University of the South in Sewanee, Tennessee, and her J.D. from the University of Tennessee, Knoxville, in 1991.

Barbara worked for four years for the Davidson County Metropolitan Public Defender's Office in Nashville. She began her career as a general sessions attorney, handling misdemeanor trials, then she became a criminal court attorney for felony trials. Barbara was later named lead trial attorney for DUI court. In this position, she handled cases involving driving under the influence (DUI), vehicular homicide, and aggravated assault.

Barbara describes the early days of her career: "One of the first things I ever did at the public defender's office was investigate a triple homicide. I had to review the crime scene photos, autopsies, and then do extensive interviews with the defendant and his family. I could've written a book on how to create a killer!"

Working as a public defender was not boring. According to Barbara, "A public defender's life is thrilling, exciting, stressful, thankless, impossible, and wonderful—all rolled into one."

Barbara regularly worked forty-five to fifty-five hours a week as a general sessions attorney. Her typical day began with a court docket containing fifteen to twenty-five names of defendants. These were Barbara's clients for the day, many of whom she would meet for the first time in court. She would confer with each client and later meet with the district attorneys. The latter meetings would determine whether Barbara marked cases for trial, for a bond-reduction hearing, for a plea-bargain offer, or for a bind-over hearing.

Barbara's workday did not end until all of the cases on her docket were disposed of. On a given day, she was responsible for all of the hearings, trials, and pleas for the public defender's office.

As a criminal attorney, Barbara was usually in court three days a week, spending two days on trials and one on motions and hearings. She handled every aspect of a client's felony case, including arraignment, research, investigation, pretrial motions, bond issues, and trial. Criminal court is less hectic than general sessions but usually involves more serious cases. Unlike general sessions court, where most trials are held before a judge only, most criminal cases are tried before a jury.

DUI court was much the same as criminal court. In this position, Barbara was responsible for approximately two hundred active cases, including probation violations. Again, she spent two or three days a week in court and averaged one jury trial per week.

Barbara talks about the positive and negative aspects of the job: "The work atmosphere in public defense is high pressure, confrontational, and intense, but very exciting. What I liked most was the enormous amount of courtroom work. If you like litigation, it's the place to be.

"What I disliked most was fighting the stereotype that public defenders are lousy lawyers simply because they work for indigent clients," Barbara recalls. "In fact, in most cases, the opposite is true. Most of the public defenders I know are exceptional attorneys. Like me, they graduated in the top part of their class and do this type of work because they enjoy it, not because they couldn't get any other job.

"The main difference between a public defender and a hired attorney is the amount of money available for expert witnesses, tests, exhibits, and the like.

"The other difference is the huge workload a public defender handles. A private attorney will have one client for the day; I may have twenty! The quality of the attorney is essentially the same, however."

Barbara no longer works as a public defender; she is now in private practice. When her children are older, she plans to return to full-time criminal practice.

"I found it very difficult to keep up the relentless pace of public defense work and be a mother. Sometimes I would have to go across town in the middle of the night for an interview or downtown to the Criminal Justice Center for a lineup or interrogation. I decided that while my children were young, I needed to stay home for a few years. I really miss the work, but it was difficult on my family."

**How Barbara Arrants Got Started.** "I went to law school because—let's face it—a liberal arts degree means I have a good education but no qualifications for anything. While applying for law school and taking the LSATs, I worked as a runner for a large firm here in Nashville. I became acquainted with all the different types of law there are, what one actually did as a lawyer, and so forth. I came away with the feeling that I did not want to be an associate in a firm. All associates do is the partners' paperwork. That did not appeal to me at all. I wanted to be in the thick of things!"

Attending a mock trial competition during her first year of law school confirmed Barbara's decision to practice criminal law. In her second year, she took a trial advocacy course and scored the highest grade in the class. The professor suggested that Barbara pursue a career in litigation.

Barbara describes her attraction to the work: "Criminal law appeals to me because of my psychology background—what makes people do the things they do? Why does someone become a criminal? I could have been a prosecutor or a defense attorney— I fell into the defense side simply because someone told me the public defenders were always looking for interns. I interned with public defense and was offered a job before I had finished my second year. Never one to look a gift horse in the mouth, I jumped on it."

**Advice from Barbara Arrants.** Barbara offers some sound advice for anyone considering a career in criminal law: "If you are interested in litigation, a job as a public defender or district attorney gets you more experience at a faster pace than any other career choice. If you start your career with a firm, you can expect to wait as long as five years before you see the inside of a courtroom. I handled my first bench trial the first week I was working! It is incredibly demanding but very rewarding as well."

## M. J. Goodwin, Family Law Attorney

M. J. Goodwin has a B.A. in modern languages and a minor in business from Clemson University in South Carolina. She received her J.D. from the University of South Carolina in Columbia in 1991.

M.J. has a private practice in Anderson, South Carolina, and business has been better than she had hoped: "I am a female solo practitioner, which makes me a minority in my town. I've done better than I ever imagined I would. I envisioned starving to death. But that hasn't happened."

M.J.'s practice covers a number of legal specialties. About 80 percent of her cases involve family law, including divorce, custody, adoption, and guardianship issues. Personal injury cases make up about 15 percent of her workload. These cases generally involve accidents, workers' compensation, and related matters. M.J. says that the remaining 5 percent is "whatever comes in the door that I think I can handle."

M.J. considers herself primarily a trial lawyer and prefers being in court to working in an office. She also has a part-time contract as the city prosecutor. In this capacity, she handles municipal-level crimes for the public defender. Most of these cases involve driving under the influence, domestic violence, or petty theft.

Workdays are defined by whatever type of case M.J. is working on. As she says, "There is no such thing as a typical day in my practice. It all depends on what kind of fire you have to put out. With domestic litigation, divorces, child custody, separations, adoptions, anything in family court—any time you're dealing with somebody's family, particularly the breakup of a marriage or a child custody dispute—well, these are the most emotionally charged kind of cases.

"I handled murder cases as a prosecutor, but these are worse than a murder case. These people are to some extent more torn up than a murder victim's family is. It's real hard to deal with people who are thinking with their emotions—and they don't realize they're doing it. They're so hurt they can't think straight. And that's what makes it stressful. Even when they win, and we have a pretty high success rate, they don't feel any better. The legal win doesn't heal the emotional scar. And I think that comes as a shock to them."

M.J.'s work involves a good deal of time out of the office. She meets with clients and is in court nearly every day, filing summonses and complaints, affidavits, and financial declarations. In her work, M.J. has more client contact than she would in other civil litigation.

She describes the difference: "If you get a car-wreck case, the client comes in and you get the medical report and take the deposition and maybe have one or two meetings. But with domestic clients, they're in almost every day because they're so upset. If they have children, it's particularly difficult for them to separate themselves from their spouses—there are always visitations and exchanges, and there is always some kind of fussing going on there."

M.J. likes the autonomy of having her own practice. Aside from court dates and appointments, she can make her own schedule. The reverse side of that, however, is that as sole proprietor, she is responsible for everything in her practice. As she says, "If something needs to be done Saturday night, I'm going to be the one to do it."

M.J. talks about how her profession lets her help others: "There's a lot of satisfaction in helping people. The legal system is complicated, and helping people get through that, however it's going to be resolved, is rewarding. Not everyone gets a good verdict; not everyone wins.

"I do a lot of pro bono cases. When I left the prosecutor's office, I made a public commitment to try to continue helping battered women. I called the newspapers, and I told them that I would help women who were staying in the shelter, that I would cut my hourly rate and let them make payments. I think that once someone has gone to the shelter, she's made enough of a commitment to get out. I had prosecuted these cases before. I think I can help more now.

"So many of these women refuse to prosecute; they just want to get away. So I try to help with their divorces. But you have a horrible problem with a lot of them going back into the marriages. Everyone's got to have a cause. This is my torch."

Working in private practice has made a tremendous difference in M.J.'s feelings about her work. While working for the prosecutor's office, she was unhappy and wished she had not gone to law school. "I enjoyed the work, I was still helping people, but there's a high burnout rate in prosecuting or even in defending.

"Burnout is caused by the high volume of cases pending all at the same time, the nature of the work (dealing with victimized souls and putting up with criminals), and the very low pay (as compared to private practice and larger firms). Prosecutors can't afford to put on as good a case as a well-funded defendant. A prosecutor has so many bosses to please: the immediate supervisor, the judge, the public, the victim, and the police. It's unlikely that you can please them all at the same time. And the criminal justice system is so far behind. It can take forever to get to trial. That adds to the frustration.

"And prosecutors are almost always in the spotlight, even in a small town. I can remember being in the paper and on TV a lot, and I found that stressful.

"But now I'm very happy. It's very different to be your own boss."

**How M. J. Goodwin Got Started.** Practicing law was not M.J.'s original goal. She was planning to study for a master's degree in French when she was called for jury duty. That experience changed everything.

"I was absolutely fascinated, mesmerized. After that I started sending to law schools for information. I was a junior at Clemson at the time. Law school will take any major, so I didn't have to change mine."

M.J.'s first job after law school was as an assistant prosecutor. She handled cases involving juveniles, domestic violence, and some sex crimes. In 1994, after three years as an assistant prosecutor, M.J. opened her own firm.

**Advice from M. J. Goodwin.** M.J. offers this advice about the practical side of the profession: "Don't do this with the idea you're going to get rich. It's a big misconception. The prosecutor jobs around here, for example, pay between $32,000 and $40,000 a year. You can make more working in a big bank.

"The large firms pay very well, but they expect sixty to seventy-five hours a week.

"In my solo practice, how I get paid depends on what kind of case it is. For domestic work I charge by the hour . . . because contingency fees in divorce cases are prohibited by our code of ethics. You wouldn't want an attorney pushing someone not to settle a case so they could get a bigger fee. For some cases, such as car wrecks, I can work on contingency, and for criminal cases I get a flat fee up front.

"It's a good idea to think very carefully about a career in law before you set out. Most people have to borrow money to go to law school.

"Also, I would suggest getting a job in a law firm before making the decision to go to law school. A lot of lawyers are very difficult to get along with and work for, and you need to be aware of all the stresses involved before you get into it.

"Becoming a lawyer is a big decision," Barbara admits. "I don't think anyone should jump into it thinking that they're, one, automatically going to get a job, or two, going to make a lot of money."

# John Wiorek, Research Attorney

John Wiorek graduated law school summa cum laude and was editor of his school's law review. He is a research attorney (formerly called a law clerk) with the Illinois Appellate Court. He is also a part-time faculty member in the Law Enforcement and Justice Administration Program at Western Illinois University in Macomb, Illinois.

The duties of a research attorney vary depending on the judge he or she works for. In John's case, writing and research are his primary duties. The appellate court handles both civil and criminal appeals. These are cases in which the attorneys are appealing the decision reached in the original trial. Attorneys submit written arguments, called briefs, which are then reviewed by the appellate court. The research attorneys must also review the transcripts of the original court proceedings.

John describes the process of preparing for an appeal. "In Illinois each appellate judge gets two law clerks, so usually the other clerk and I will split up the work. We know what cases are set for the particular month, and we have all of these stacks of briefs to read. The three of us—the other law clerk, the judge, and I—make notes on the briefs and arguments. This could take three or four days. "Then we have a conference and go through each case and discuss it. We give the judge our ideas on how the case should turn out.

"At the same time, we begin to research the law regarding those cases. We might work up a rough draft of decisions and do bench memos for other cases—giving a brief synopsis of the arguments and the law and what our feelings are about what the decision should or shouldn't be.

"The judge will listen to the oral arguments and come back and tell us what was decided, whether the original judgment was affirmed or reversed, and he'll explain the reasons for how the court reached the decision. We will then write a draft of the order."

The work of a research attorney is not as stressful as some of the other court positions described earlier. As John says, "Any stress on the job would be mostly self-imposed. There are no hard-and-fast deadlines, although you do have to produce a certain amount of work in a certain amount of time. No judge likes to get behind on the caseload.

John's workday is eight hours, from nine to five. The regular schedule keeps the stress level low and allows John to pursue other interests. He is able to teach a night course at Western Illinois University and can do independent work for clients.

The downside, for John, is the potential for the work to be tedious. "Sometimes the work can get a bit repetitious—the issues can recur and they can be boring. Sometimes you read a two-thousand-page transcript and you're sitting there for three days reading some psychiatrist giving you his opinion about someone's sanity and going through the results of his MMPI and different psychological tests. It can get tedious."

Overall, though, John sees the positive side of the job: "There is a certain satisfaction when you're done with a case, especially if the judges decide to make it an opinion rather than an order, which means it will be published. You can see in the books that you made a small contribution to developing the law."

**How John Wiorek Got Started.** The legal profession was not John's first career choice. As he says, "My decision to go into law came primarily from finding out after graduating with a bachelor's in psychology that the options were fairly limited with that kind of degree. So I spent some time kicking around a little bit, trying to decide the best route to go—a doctorate in psychology or law school. Although I had no great burning desire to go into law, law school seemed like the best option, something I'd be good at—based on my LSAT results—and something I thought had a fairly good potential for a job."

John earned his B.S. from Western Illinois University in Macomb in 1978. He attended law school at Southern Illinois University in Carbondale and graduated in 1988 with a J.D.

John's first job after law school was as a staff attorney on the Fifth District Appellate Court in Mt. Vernon, Illinois. Six months later he began working as a law clerk.

"Most of the time law clerk positions are temporary; one or two years is the norm. It is seen more as a stepping-stone to something else rather than as a career in itself. In fact, the reason I no longer work for the first judge is that he basically said to me, 'OK, your two years are up, and it's time for you to move on to something else.' He thought I should be doing something 'better' for my career.

"I chose to continue as a law clerk with another judge because I found that I liked this kind of work, that I was good at it, and that I was comfortable with it. I didn't want to work with a firm. There are so many horror stories. The eighty-hour weeks. The grind. It didn't appeal to me at all. My job is nine to five. I get a steady paycheck; I know how much it's going to be. I don't work weekends or nights, and the stress level is really low."

**Advice from John Wiorek.** John's advice is to be well prepared for work as a law clerk: "There are certain qualifications you have to have. If you want to be a law clerk, you're going to have to finish in at least the top quarter or probably the top 10 percent of your class. They're going to want you to have good grades or be on the law review.

"Also, you have to be able to write and like to write. If it's a real chore for you, it won't be the right job for you. Your analytical skills have to be fairly high, too.

"I would advise anyone to go for being a law clerk for at least one to two years. If you're thinking about making it a career, there are a couple of things to keep in mind. You'll make less money than in a firm. Plus, the job security isn't there. You serve at the whim of the judge you work for. He could retire or quit or not get reelected, and then you're out of a job.

"Another point is to make sure you take a job with a judge you like and get along with. You spend a lot of time working closely together, so that's important. I'm lucky. I have a good judge to work for."

# CHAPTER THREE

# Judges

Judges apply the law and oversee the legal process in courts according to local, state, and federal statutes. They preside over cases concerning every aspect of society, including traffic offenses, disputes over the management of professional sports, issues concerning the rights of huge corporations, and questions regarding the rights of the terminally ill when disconnecting life-support equipment. Judges must ensure that trials and hearings are conducted fairly and that the court administers justice in a manner that safeguards the legal rights of all parties involved.

The most visible responsibility of judges is presiding over trials or hearings and listening as attorneys represent the parties present. Judges rule on the admissibility of evidence and the methods of conducting testimony, and they may be called upon to settle disputes between opposing attorneys. They also ensure that rules and procedures are followed, and if unusual circumstances arise for which standard procedures have not been established, they interpret the law and determine the manner in which the trial will proceed.

Judges often hold pretrial hearings for cases. They listen to allegations and determine whether the evidence presented merits a trial. In criminal cases, judges may decide that persons charged with crimes should be held in jail pending trial, or they may set the conditions for their release. In civil cases, they occasionally impose restrictions upon the parties until a trial is held.

In many trials, juries are selected to decide guilt or innocence in criminal cases or liability and compensation in civil cases. Judges instruct juries on applicable laws, direct them to deduce the facts from the evidence presented, and hear their verdict. When the law does not require a jury trial or when the parties waive their right to a jury, judges decide the cases.

Judges also work outside the courtroom, "in chambers." In their private offices, judges read documents on pleadings and motions, research legal issues, write opinions, and oversee the court's operations. In some jurisdictions, judges also manage the administrative and clerical staff of the court.

## Types of Judges

Judges' duties vary according to the extent of their jurisdictions and powers.

- **General trial court judges** of the federal and state court systems have jurisdiction over any case in their system. They usually try civil cases transcending the jurisdiction of lower courts and all cases involving felony offenses.
- **Appellate court judges** on both the federal and state level, although few in number, have the power to overrule decisions made by trial court or administrative law judges if they determine that legal errors were made in a case or if legal precedent does not support the judgment of the lower court. Appellate court judges rule on a small number of cases and rarely have direct contacts with litigants. Instead, they usually base their decisions on lower court records and lawyers' written and oral arguments.
- Many **state court judges** preside in courts whose jurisdiction is limited by law to certain types of cases. The various titles assigned to these judges include **municipal court judge**, **county court judge**, **magistrate**, and **justice of the peace**. Traffic violations, misdemeanors, small-claims cases, and pretrial hearings constitute the bulk of the work of state court judges, but some states allow them to

handle cases involving domestic relations, probate, contracts, and other selected areas of the law.

- **Administrative law judges**, sometimes called **hearing officers** or **adjudicators**, are employed by government agencies to make determinations for administrative agencies. They make decisions, for example, on eligibility for various Social Security or workers' compensation benefits, on protection of the environment, on the enforcement of health and safety regulations, on employment discrimination, and on compliance with economic regulatory requirements.

## Working Conditions

Judges do most of their work in offices, law libraries, and courtrooms. The work presents few hazards, although sitting in the same position in the courtroom for long periods can be tiring. Most judges wear robes when they are in a courtroom.

Judges typically work a standard forty-hour week, but many work more than fifty. Some judges with limited jurisdiction are employed part-time and divide their time between their judicial responsibilities and other careers.

## Training for Judges

A bachelor's degree and work experience usually constitute the minimum requirement for a judgeship. A number of lawyers become judges, and most judges have first been lawyers. In fact, federal and state judges usually are required to be lawyers. About forty states allow nonlawyers to hold limited-jurisdiction judgeships, but opportunities are better for those with law experience. Federal administrative law judges must be lawyers and pass a competitive examination administered by the U.S. Office of Personnel Management. Some state administrative law judges and other hearing officials are not required to be lawyers.

Federal administrative law judges are appointed by various federal agencies and virtually have lifetime tenure. Federal magistrate judges are appointed by district judges—the life-tenured federal judges of a district court—to serve eight years in a U.S. district court. A part-time federal magistrate's term of office is four years.

Some state judges are appointed, but the remainder are elected in partisan or nonpartisan state elections. Many state and local judges serve fixed renewable terms ranging from four or six years for some trial court judgeships to as long as fourteen years or even life for other trial or appellate court judges. Judicial nominating commissions, composed of members of the bar and the public, are used to screen candidates for judgeships in many states and for some federal judgeships.

All states have some type of orientation for newly elected or appointed judges. The Federal Judicial Center, American Bar Association, National Judicial College, and National Center for State Courts provide judicial education and training for judges and other judicial-branch personnel. General and continuing education courses usually last from a couple of days to three weeks. More than half of all states, as well as Puerto Rico, require judges to enroll in continuing education courses while serving on the bench.

## Judges in Canada

Eligibility requirements for judges vary among the provinces. In general, a prospective judge must have extensive experience as a lawyer or a professor of law, with continuous membership in the bar association.

Judges must be members in good standing of a provincial or territorial law society or bar association. Federally appointed judges must be lawyers who have been members of a provincial bar for ten years.

Provincial or municipal governments appoint judges to provincial lower courts. These judges handle both provincial and federal cases. Judges of both the Supreme Court and Federal Court are appointed by the federal government, which also appoints some provincial judges.

## Job Outlook

Employment of judges is expected to grow more slowly than the average through 2012. Budgetary pressures at all levels of government will restrict the hiring of judges, despite rising caseloads, particularly in federal courts. Most job openings will arise as judges retire. However, additional openings may occur when new judgeship positions are authorized by law or when judges are elevated to a higher judicial office.

Public concerns about crime and safety, as well as a public increasingly willing to go to court to settle disputes, should spur demand for judges. Not only has the quantity of a judge's work increased, but many cases have become more complex because of developments in information technology, medical science, e-commerce, and globalization.

The prestige associated with serving on the bench should ensure competition for judge and magistrate positions. However, a growing number of judges and candidates for judgeships are choosing to forgo the bench and work in the private sector, where pay is significantly higher. This movement may lessen the competition somewhat. In addition, judicial candidates frequently must gain political support in order to be elected or appointed, and getting that support can be expensive, which may limit the number of potential candidates competing for judgeships.

## Employment Figures

Judges, magistrates, and magistrate judges held twenty-seven thousand jobs in 2002, primarily in state and local government. Administrative law judges, adjudicators, and hearing officers held about nineteen thousand jobs; 57 percent worked in state governments, 24 percent in the federal government, and 16 percent in local governments. Arbitrators, mediators, and conciliators held another sixty-one hundred jobs. Approximately half worked for state and local governments. The remainder worked for labor organizations, law offices, insurance carriers, and other private companies and for organizations that specialize in providing dispute resolution services.

# Earnings

Judges, magistrate judges, and magistrates had median annual earnings of $94,070 in 2002. The middle 50 percent earned between $44,970 and $120,390. The top 10 percent earned more than $138,300, while the bottom 10 percent earned less than $24,250.

Median annual earnings in the industries employing the largest numbers of judges, magistrate judges, and magistrates in 2002 were $112,720 in state government and $54,750 in local government. Administrative law judges, adjudicators, and hearing officers earned a median of $64,540.

The chief justice of the United States Supreme Court earned $198,600 in 2001, and the associate justices earned $190,100. Federal court of appeals judges earned $164,100 a year, while district court judges had salaries of $154,700, as did judges in the Court of Federal Claims and the Court of International Trade. Federal judges with limited jurisdiction, such as magistrates and bankruptcy court judges, had salaries of $142,324.

According to a survey by the National Center for State Courts, annual salaries of associate justices of state high courts averaged $120,100 in 2002 and ranged from about $89,381 to $170,319. Salaries of state intermediate appellate court judges averaged $116,064 and ranged from $91,469 to $159,657. Salaries of state judges with general jurisdiction trial courts averaged $109,811 and ranged from $82,600 to $150,000. Most salaried judges are provided health and life insurance, and contributions to retirement plans are made on their behalf.

.......................................................

# What It's Really Like

## James Lanuti, Circuit Court Judge

James Lanuti earned his J.D. at Illinois Institute of Technology–Chicago Kent College of Law in 1977. He is a judge in the circuit court of LaSalle County in Illinois.

Judge Lanuti hears civil cases, such as divorces, paternity suits, lawsuits, personal injury, and contract disputes. He also handles probate matters, estate law, and will contests.

In his words, "I've handled just about everything. When I first went on the bench I did a lot of divorces cases. Then I spent four years doing traffic court, where I heard the traffic cases as well as all the drunk driving cases, the serious traffic cases as well as reckless homicide cases, where people have been killed in drunk driving accidents, and some felonies—people charged with more serious crimes.

"At the same time I also heard the cases that are the most distressing—juvenile cases. I was the presiding judge of the juvenile court where I heard all the juvenile delinquency cases as well as cases involving abused and neglected children. I did that for about four years. Then I came back and did another stretch of civil cases. I was also in charge of probate cases for a while."

Judge Lanuti was assigned to criminal court, where he worked for more than three years. He then requested a transfer to civil court, wanting something different. "I was ready for a little change. I heard only murder cases, armed robbery, and so forth. It would be ideal to get a variety of criminal and civil cases, but in my county we separate the two."

Judge Lanuti's caseload varies daily, with a lot depending on how the cases are disposed of. As he says, "If everything were litigated, you couldn't hear more than one case in a day. In an average day you might have thirty cases on your docket, but they all go away because they get settled. On another day you might only have half a dozen on the docket, but that might be a day you're in court all day because most of the cases are contested."

On a typical day the judge arrives at court by 8 A.M. to prepare for his first court call at 9 A.M. If the cases are easily resolved, he might finish in court by 3 in the afternoon; otherwise he is there until 5 P.M.

A shorter court day doesn't mean that Judge Lanuti's workday is over, however. "When I finish court early, I can use the time in chambers to familiarize myself with the next day's call. When I was a lawyer, I always appreciated a judge who took the time to be prepared, to read the papers that the lawyers had filed. That isn't always the case, but that's one thing as a judge I've always shot for, and to do it requires a certain amount of homework. You have to read the files, read the motions and the answers, and do some research.

"We don't have interns or law clerks, but we do have a circuit clerk who is basically the record keeper and does the scheduling, like a clerk of the court. We do our own research."

Judge Lanuti talks about the ups and downs of the job: "Obviously, the work is very interesting. It's not boring at all, and you see a lot of situations where you think you can make a difference. You can't always make everyone happy, though. Your first and foremost job is to follow the law. Sometimes that's not popular, but as long as you can do it consistently, it will give you a sense of satisfaction. You're doing your part to administer justice.

"It can be frustrating sometimes if you end up having to hear cases that really should have been resolved before they came to court. You see a lot of people who are almost self-destructive. I see that a lot in divorce cases, like the movie *War of the Roses*. That's not totally untrue. And the saddest thing about it is to see the effect it has on children.

"That's one of the things we've tried to focus on in recent years in the court system on a national level. What can the courts do to make sure the children don't get lost in the shuffle? You have to realize, though, that the litigants have ultimate control over their own lives. You can't solve all of society's social problems. Even though you'd like to be able to get people to listen, sometimes they won't take your advice.

"It's also frustrating to see a juvenile come in, charged with a crime. You try to work with him—you talk to him, maybe give him probation and all sorts of other services. It's sad to see him come back a couple of years later charged with a felony as an adult who's going to go to prison.

"Once in a while you might worry about a decision on a tough case, but not often. I've felt comfortable with most of the decisions I've made. You have to have the ability to put the case behind you or else you won't be effective."

**How James Lanuti Got Started.** James earned a B.S. in math at the University of Illinois. He then worked for seven years as a computer program systems analyst, continuing to work at night while he attended law school. Becoming a judge was not, however, his intention: "My goal at the time was to be able to work for myself and be independent, and I saw the law as a way to do that. I never intended at the time I started law school to become a judge. That was never a goal."

James worked for a Chicago law firm and then moved to Ottawa, Illinois, because he had relatives in the area. He began working with his uncle, who is an attorney in Ottawa. In addition, he worked for the state attorney's office as a part-time assistant state attorney. In this position, he handled civil matters and represented the county government in cases.

James describes how he became a judge: "The way the system works in the state of Illinois is that we have two levels of trial judges: associate judges and circuit judges. The associate judges are appointed by the circuit judges for four-year terms. Circuit judges are elected for six-year terms. The circuit judges have to run for retention on a yes/no ballot every six years.

"In 1986 there was a judicial vacancy for an associate judge, and I talked about it with my family and thought, 'Why not give it a try? If I don't get it, I won't look back and worry about it.' But I got appointed.

"Whenever there's a vacancy for an associate judge, a notice is posted at the courthouse and any lawyer can apply. Then all the circuit judges meet and vote via secret ballot.

"I knew the circuit judges at that point. That's one of the strong points of the system. The same lawyers who apply appear in the courtroom in front of the same judges who vote, so the judges already have a pretty good idea of the capabilities of the lawyers."

**Advice from James Lanuti.** Judge Lanuti offers this advice for those who are interested in serving as judges: "I don't think you start off considering a career as a judge. First, you decide if you want to get into the law, and if you want to be a lawyer, that's a career you choose. Once you're practicing law you'd know more about judges and know whether that's what you'd want to do.

"Some people are designed to be advocates—they can advocate a position strongly, even though the position might not be a good one. They don't judge their own clients. The client comes in and says, 'This is the position I want to take in this case,' and the lawyer says, 'It's not unreasonable, so let's go ahead with it.' Other lawyers, though, might be more judgmental. They might say, 'Come on, Mr. Client, we'll never sell this to the jury. Let's compromise.' You see the practical route and the outcome, and you're not wearing blinders just to advocate your client's position. If that's the way you operate, it might be an indication that you're better off being a judge.

"It's a steady position. You'll make a good living, and you have a certain amount of freedom in the job. You're in charge of your docket, and you're the one making the decisions. You can have some control with what's going on in front of you with the lawyers, and you get the holidays and the weekends off.

"But the idea of being your own boss is something you have to give up when you're a judge because now you're a public servant. You're no longer working for yourself; you're working for the public, and you have an obligation to be at work and be on the job.

"And though you do make a good living, you are giving up the opportunity to make substantially more as a lawyer. There are lawyers, obviously, who don't make as much money as judges, but there are many lawyers who make a lot more."

# CHAPTER FOUR

# Court Staff

I n addition to the obvious personnel you see buzzing around the courtroom—the lawyers and their staff and the judges—there are other key personnel who keep the court running smoothly. Among these are court clerks, court reporters, and bailiffs.

## Clerks of the Court

Court clerks administer the day-to-day dealings in courts of law. They oversee a staff of legal and administrative personnel who perform a variety of duties, such as preparing dockets of cases to be called; securing information for judges; and contacting witnesses, attorneys, and litigants to obtain information for court. Some clerks of the court are elected, and others are appointed, depending on the state and the level of the court. Court, municipal, and license clerks held 106,000 jobs in 2002.

### Training for Clerks of the Court

Although being an attorney is not a requirement for a clerk of the court position, more and more judges are preferring to work with experienced clerks who have more than administrative skills. The trend has been for attorneys to be given preference for clerk positions over other applicants.

The training and educational requirements for attorneys are covered in Chapter 2.

## Job Outlook

As more and more courts are established to handle the increase in cases, more positions for clerks of the court will be opening. However, job openings will occur primarily to replace existing workers who retire, and the competition for these positions will remain keen.

## Earnings

Salaries for clerks of the court vary widely—from $40,000 to $80,000 per year—depending upon the region of the country and the level of the court.

# Court Reporters

Court reporters typically take verbatim reports of speeches, conversations, legal proceedings, meetings, and other events when written accounts of spoken words are necessary for correspondence, records, or legal proof.

In addition to preparing and protecting the legal record, many court reporters assist judges and trial attorneys in a variety of ways, such as organizing and searching for information in the official record or making suggestions to judges and attorneys regarding courtroom administration and procedure.

Court reporters play a critical role not only in judicial proceedings, but at every meeting where the spoken word must be preserved as a written transcript. They are responsible for ensuring a complete, accurate, and secure legal record. There are two main methods of court reporting: stenotyping and voice writing.

## Stenotypists

Using a stenotype machine, stenotypists document all statements made in official proceedings. The machine allows them to press multiple keys to record combinations of letters that represent sounds, words, or phrases. These symbols are then recorded on computer disks or CD-ROM, then translated and displayed as text in a process called computer-aided transcription. In all cases, accuracy is crucial because there is only one person creating an official transcript. In a judicial setting, for example, the outcome of an appeal often depends on the court reporter's transcript.

Stenotype machines used for real-time captioning are linked directly to a computer. As the reporter keys in the symbols, they instantly appear as text on the screen. This process, called communications access real-time translation (CART), is used in courts, in classrooms, at meetings, and for closed captioning for the hearing impaired on television.

## Voice Writers

The other method of court reporting is called voice writing. Using the voice-writing method, a court reporter speaks directly into a stenomask—a hand-held mask containing a microphone with a voice silencer. As the reporter repeats the testimony into the recorder, the mask and silencer prevent the reporter from being heard during testimony. Voice writers record everything that is said by judges, witnesses, attorneys, and other parties to a proceeding, including gestures and emotional reactions.

Some voice writers produce a transcript in real time, using computer speech recognition technology. Other voice writers prefer to translate their voice files after the proceeding is over, or they transcribe the files manually, without using speech recognition at all. In any event, speech recognition technology is allowing voice writers to pursue not only court reporting careers, but also careers as closed captioners, CART reporters for hearing-impaired individuals, and providers of Internet streaming text or captions.

## Working Conditions

Although many court reporters record official proceedings in the courtroom, others work outside the courtroom. For example, they may take depositions for attorneys in offices and document proceedings of meetings, conventions, and other private activities. Still others capture the proceedings taking place in government agencies at all levels, from the U.S. Congress to state and local governing bodies. Increasingly, court reporters provide closed-captioning and real-time translating services to the deaf and hard-of-hearing community.

Court reporters, both stenotypists and voice writers, who specialize in captioning live television programming for people with hearing loss are commonly known as stenocaptioners. They work for television networks or cable stations, captioning news, emergency broadcasts, sporting events, and other programming. With CART and broadcast captioning, the quality and accuracy of the information presented to a person with hearing loss depends solely on the skill of the stenocaptioner. In an emergency, such as a tornado or a hurricane, people's safety may depend entirely on the accuracy of information provided in the form of captioning.

## Training for Court Reporters

The training required to become a court reporter varies with the type of reporting. It usually takes less than a year to become a voice writer. In contrast, it takes thirty-three months, on average, to become a stenotypist. Training is offered by about 160 postsecondary vocational and technical schools and colleges. The National Court Reporters Association (NCRA) has approved eighty-two programs, all of which offer courses in stenotyping, computer-aided transcription, and real-time reporting. NCRA-approved programs require students to capture a minimum of 225 words per minute, a federal government requirement as well.

Some states require court reporters to be notary publics. Others require the Certified Court Reporter (CCR) designation, for which a reporter must pass a state certification test administered by a board of examiners. The NCRA confers the entry-level designation Registered Professional Reporter (RPR) upon those who pass a four-part examination and participate in mandatory continuing education programs. Although voluntary, the designation is recognized as a mark of distinction in the field.

A reporter may obtain additional certifications that demonstrate higher levels of competency, such as the Registered Merit Reporter (RMR) or Registered Diplomate Reporter (RDR) designations. The RDR is the highest level of certification available to court reporters. In order to receive the designation, a court reporter must either have five consecutive years of experience as an RMR or be an RMR and hold a four-year baccalaureate degree.

The NCRA also offers the designations Certified Realtime Reporter (CRR), Certified Broadcast Captioner (CBC), and Certified CART Provider (CCP). These designations promote and recognize competence in the specialized skill of converting the spoken word into the written word instantaneously.

Some states require voice writers to pass a test and to earn state licensure. As a substitute for state certification, the National Verbatim Reporters Association offers three national certifications to voice writers: Certified Verbatim Reporter (CVR), the Certificate of Merit (CM), and Realtime Verbatim Reporter (RVR). Earning these certifications may be sufficient to get licensed in the state. In order to get the CM or RVR, one must first earn the CVR.

Candidates for the CVR must pass a written test covering punctuation, spelling, grammar, legal terminology, definitions, and more and also must pass three five-minute dictation and transcription examinations that test for speed as well as accuracy.

Passing the CM exam requires a higher level of speed and accuracy. The RVR measures the candidate's skill at real-time transcription. In order to retain these certifications, the voice writer must obtain continuing education credits. Credits are given for voice writer education courses, continuing legal education courses, and college courses.

In addition to possessing speed and accuracy, court reporters must have excellent listening skills, as well as solid grammar, vocabulary, and punctuation skills. Voice writers must learn to listen and speak simultaneously and very quickly while also identifying speakers and describing peripheral activities in the courtroom or deposition room. They must be aware of business practices and current events as well as the correct spelling of the names of people, places, and events that may be mentioned in a broadcast or in court proceedings.

For those who work in courtrooms, an expert knowledge of legal terminology and criminal and appellate procedure is essential. Because capturing proceedings requires the use of computerized stenography or speech recognition equipment, court reporters must be knowledgeable about computer hardware and software applications.

With experience and education, court reporters can advance to administrative and management positions, consulting, or teaching.

## Employment Figures

Court reporters held about eighteen thousand jobs in 2002. About 60 percent worked for state and local governments, a reflection of the large number of court reporters working in courts, legislatures, and various agencies. Most of the remaining wage and salary employees worked for court reporting agencies. Roughly 11 percent of court reporters were self-employed.

## Job Outlook

Employment of court reporters is projected to grow about as fast as the average for all occupations through 2012. Demand for court reporter services will be spurred by the continuing need for accurate transcription of proceedings in courts and in pretrial depositions and by the growing need to create captions for live or prerecorded television and to provide other real-time translating services for the deaf and hard-of-hearing community.

Despite the good job prospects, fewer people are entering this profession, which is creating a serious shortage of court reporters, particularly stenographic typists, therefore making job opportunities good to excellent. Because of this shortage, voice writers have become more widely accepted as speech-recognition technology improves and error rates decline. Still, many courts hire only stenotypists to perform court reporting duties, and because of this practice, demand for these highly skilled reporters will remain high.

Federal legislation mandates that by 2006, all new television programming must be captioned for the deaf and hard-of-hearing. In addition, the Americans with Disabilities Act gives deaf and hard-of-hearing students in colleges and universities the right to request access to real-time translation in their classes. Both of these factors are expected to increase demand for court reporters to provide real-time captioning and CART services. Although these services differ from traditional court reporting, which uses computer-aided transcription to turn spoken words into permanent text, they require the same skills that court reporters learn in their training.

Despite increasing numbers of civil and criminal cases, budget constraints are expected to limit the ability of federal, state, and local courts to expand, thereby also limiting the demand for traditional court reporting services in courtrooms and other legal venues. Many courtrooms, in an effort to keep costs down, have installed tape recorders to maintain records of proceedings, but some jurisdictions have found the error rates associated with tape recorders to be unacceptable, bringing court reporters back to their courtrooms despite budgetary issues. Court reporters can quickly turn spoken words into readable, searchable, permanent text; therefore, they will continue to be needed to produce written legal transcripts and proceedings for publication.

## Earnings

Court reporters had median annual earnings of $41,550 in 2002. The middle 50 percent earned between $29,770 and $55,360. The lowest-paid 10 percent earned less than $23,120, and the highest-paid 10 percent earned more than $73,440. For the court reporters working in local government, median annual earnings were $40,720.

Both the amount and the methods of compensation for court reporters vary with the type of reporting job, the experience of the individual reporter, the level of certification achieved, and the region of the country the reporter works in. Official court reporters earn a salary as well as a per-page fee for transcripts.

Many salaried court reporters supplement their income by doing additional freelance work. Freelance court reporters are paid per job and receive a per-page fee for transcripts. Communication access real-time translation providers are paid hourly. Stenocaptioners receive a salary and benefits if they work as employees of a captioning company; stenocaptioners working as independent contractors are paid hourly.

## Bailiffs

Bailiffs are responsible for maintaining order in a courtroom. They enforce rules of behavior and provide security. At the beginning of their shifts, they check courtrooms to make sure they are safe. They look for concealed guns, bombs, or other safety hazards.

Bailiffs announce the entrance of judges into courtrooms. They prevent people from entering courtrooms while judges are instructing juries. They also make sure people watching trials do not talk to the jury. Bailiffs inform people of courtroom rules and enforce those rules; they may remove or arrest people who do not cooperate. In addition, they restrain observers who act aggressively when they dislike decisions. If needed, bailiffs contact the sheriff's office for help. In case of medical emergencies, they contact medical staff.

In many trials that last more than one day, judges decide that jurors cannot return to their homes until trials are over. In these situations, jurors must stay at hotels. Bailiffs guard these hotels and escort jurors to restaurants to keep the public from contacting them.

In addition to security services, bailiffs also swear in witnesses, handle articles of evidence, and escort prisoners to and from court. They also ensure that judges have case files and supplies.

Depending on the judge or the court system in which the bailiff works, he or she may have additional duties, including administrative tasks, such as preparing the docket for the next day's cases, serving writs and subpoenas, and handling evictions or repossessions.

## Training for Bailiffs

A high school diploma or GED is the minimum requirement for this occupation. However, many bailiffs have training beyond high school. Many have a degree in law enforcement or criminal justice. Some community colleges and universities offer these programs. Some bailiffs also have experience as sheriff's deputies or police officers.

Many states require all law enforcement officers, including bailiffs, to complete Peace Officer Standards and Training Academy (POST). New officers attend police academies for three to six months, studying laws and ordinances, self-defense, and first aid. Additional training includes handling emergency situations and proper use of weapons.

Some court systems offer formal training programs for bailiffs. Usually lasting one month, these programs teach bailiffs to protect judges and defend themselves. They are also taught procedures for handling evidence and for dealing with juries and prisoners.

## Job Outlook

Employment of bailiffs is expected to grow as fast as the average through the year 2010. All bailiffs work for the government; thus, the state of the economy should not have much impact on this occupation. The crime level is more likely to affect the number of jobs for bailiffs. If the crime level increases, more bailiffs may be needed to control the larger number of offenders. If the crime level decreases, the number of bailiffs may be reduced.

## Earnings

Median annual earnings of all bailiffs were $32,710 in 2002. The middle 50 percent earned between $22,960 and $44,280. The lowest 10 percent earned less than $16,870, and the highest 10 percent earned more than $55,270. Median annual earnings were $27,470 for bailiffs working in local government.

# What It's Really Like

### Gist Fleshman, Clerk of the Court

Gist Fleshman has a B.S. in political science from Illinois State University in Normal, Illinois. After working for a Congressman in Washington, D.C., for a couple of years, he went back to school and earned his J.D. from DePaul University in Chicago in 1985. He was appointed clerk of the court for the Illinois Appellate Court Third District in 1992.

Gist Fleshman describes his job: "My official job title is clerk of the appellate court/attorney. There are also clerks of the court who are not attorneys—it's a lower pay grade.

"The clerk of the court is the head administrative official in a court. He or she is the person who runs the court's operations on a day-to-day basis. The clerk may or may not answer to the judges, depending on the system."

According to Gist, his work is about 40 percent legal and 60 percent administrative. He manages the day-to-day operations for the court, dealing regularly with the public and the press. He handles all motions filed in the court and has been authorized to make decisions on routine motions. For more complex issues, Gist will discuss the case with the motions judge and perhaps do some research.

On the administrative side, Gist says, "It's the usual. I make sure people show up and do their job. I make some policy decisions and take care of the maintenance of the building. I supervise eighteen people: staff attorneys, the chief deputy clerk and seven deputy clerks, and the maintenance and housekeeping staff. There are six judges in the court, and each has two law clerks and one secretary."

The job provides Gist with variety. He has the opportunity to do legal work but doesn't experience too much stress in the process. As he says, "I get to do legal work, and I get to, in some ways, decide how much to do. If I don't have time I can delegate things to the research department.

"On the other hand, if it's something that's going to be a nice issue to get into and research—which is what I love to do—I can do it myself.

"At the same time I can negotiate with contractors and read blueprints and study the contracts—that sort of thing. The courthouse is an historic building, so there's always something to do there."

For Gist, the downside of the job comes from the administrative work. Personnel problems are the main issue that comes with managing a staff, and Gist has learned to deal with these issues as they arise.

The best part of the job for Gist is the possibility of helping others. "One of the things I love the most is that you can make a big difference. You definitely see injustices, where people have gotten a raw deal—people in prison who shouldn't be or children who were taken away needlessly from their parents. Unlike in other jobs, here you can do something about it. You can pick up the phone and talk to a judge and tell him what's going on. You end up being a bit of an advocate for a party. The judges listen to me. Wrongs can be righted. I love that aspect. It's very gratifying."

**How Gist Fleshman Got Started.** Gist describes how he came to work in the legal profession: "I got my degree in political science. I enjoyed that but didn't want to do it for the rest of my life. I took some time off and realized I needed more than a political science degree and something that would allow me to go right away into a job. I considered an M.B.A. or a law degree, and the law degree sounded more interesting to me. But I'm not one of these people who knew from the time they were five they wanted to be a lawyer."

Gist began working at the courthouse as a staff attorney immediately after finishing law school. He worked on the central research staff and thought he would continue in that job for one or two years, then go into private practice. He found that he enjoyed the work and stayed for two more years.

The opportunity to clerk for a couple of judges came up, along with a significant pay raise. Gist accepted that job and was soon offered the position of research director, managing the day-to-day operations of the central staff attorneys.

Gist also returned to school with the intention of pursuing patent law. As he says, "I kept thinking I'd move on, and I was preparing for that. When the clerk of the court started talking about retirement, I put in my name among the applicants, and I was chosen. That was in 1992.

"I've been here longer than any judge who's been here. That was one nice thing about going up through the ranks. The judges put a lot more trust in me than they would in someone they just hired from outside."

**Advice from Gist Fleshman.** Gist has some thoughts to share with aspiring clerks of the court: "You need to work your way up. The courts want someone with experience. Coming in as a staff attorney or law clerk is how to do it because you learn how the court works.

"And in some ways it's a position you can create for yourself because it's something that's developing. If you prove yourself and put a bug in the judge's ear, you could make the job be what you want it to be.

"But it's very competitive, and you need to make sure you have excellent reading and writing skills."

## Dan P. Clark, Court Reporter

Dan Clark is a court reporter and partner in Maffei & Clark Court Reporting Service in San Rafael, California. He has been working in the field since 1976.

Dan describes his company's business: "Maffei & Clark Court Reporting Service supplies court reporting services for the legal industry. The major thrust of our service revolves around reporting depositions; however, we also report arbitrations, examinations under oath. We have five reporters we work with. All of our reporters are on an independent-contractor basis and are not employees."

For the most part, Dan enjoys his job. On a typical day, he goes to a deposition, swears in the witness, and takes a verbatim record of what is said. While this might sound routine, it really isn't. Here is Dan's summary of his work:

"I enjoy my job—some days. It's important to remember that a deposition is usually an adversarial proceeding. Personalities can get very intense. I usually find my job interesting, as I get to go different places and meet different people every day, but occasionally I get a little bored, especially with contract law cases. Sometimes it's very, very busy and all the clients want their transcripts yesterday, and then sometimes it's slow. Depositions go on and off at the drop of the hat, so you have no idea really what days you'll actually end up working or where.

"I think the only thing that really bothers me are people who are not concerned about what kind of a record they are making,"

Gist says. "But I do get to meet a variety of people. I learn something at every deposition I take. I take depositions from people in every walk of life, from a neurosurgeon to a baker to an industrial engineer."

**How Dan Clark Got Started.** Dan completed two years of college and then attended a school for court reporters in Denver, Colorado. He is a Certified Shorthand Reporter (CSR), which is the state certification. In addition, he is nationally certified as a Registered Professional Reporter (RPR).

Dan's decision to study court reporting was made in an interesting way: "I was working as a court clerk in Denver County Court, and knew I needed to get schooling in something. I was a fairly fast typist. An attorney noticed how fast I could type and said, 'Hey, you should go to court reporting school.' My response was, 'That's exactly what I've been looking for!'"

When he finished court reporting school, Dan moved to San Francisco. He was hired by a court reporting firm, where he worked for seven years, ultimately becoming a partner. He left that firm to start his own company.

**Advice from Dan Clark.** Dan's advice for anyone interested in becoming a court reporter addresses the qualities you will need to pursue this interesting career. "Make sure you have a good background in English. You should have a curiosity about life. You should be able to concentrate. You also need good computer skills.

"Becoming a Certified Shorthand Reporter is very difficult to do. People watch us and think, 'Oh, that looks easy. They're hardly moving.' But that's not the case.

"When you go to school, don't give up. Only one-third of the people who enter court reporting school actually get out of school and become certified. Many people don't realize how very difficult it is. For example, in order to become certified in California, you must be able to write four voice testimonies at 225 words a minute. That's a real challenge!"

## Kent Reeves, Deputy Bailiff

Kent Reeves is a deputy bailiff with the Fairborn/Beavercreek Municipal Court in Fairborn, Ohio. He has two associate's degrees and a bachelor's degree in American jurisprudence from Wright State University in Dayton, Ohio. He began his current job in 1985.

Kent handles court security and some administrative tasks. He is responsible for the safety of the judge and magistrate. He puts people sentenced by the judge into holding cells and is responsible for prisoners who come to court from the jail.

The administrative part of Kent's job involves preparing cases for the following day's docket and seeing that the judge has all necessary paperwork.

As Kent says, "Our office prides itself on having the information even before the judge wants it."

In addition to these duties, Kent serves subpoenas, writs, and summonses for both criminal and civil court. He evicts tenants and, in some cases, repossesses property.

Reflecting on all of these duties, Kent says, "Most of the time my job is not too dangerous; however, it does have its moments. Every now and then, we must chase after escaped prisoners or try to serve someone or obtain real property from someone who does not want to be cooperative.

"We wear suits and ties in the court. After hours we can wear anything. A lot of times I come home to change into jeans and a T-shirt when I go out to serve papers. It's more comfortable and also a lot of people will be more responsive than if they see a 'suit' coming up their walk.

"I think my favorite part of my job is the interaction that I have with a variety of people. I try to treat people the way I would want to be treated if our roles were reversed. By doing this, most everyone responds positively. And even when I have to lock peo-ple up, they usually don't give me any problems.

"The thing I dislike most is that being around a certain element of society all day sometimes makes me cynical and distrustful."

**How Kent Reeves Got Started.** When he finished high school, Kent wanted to be a lawyer. By the time he graduated from college, however, he had changed his mind: "I came to the conclusion that I could not defend the ones I thought were guilty, nor could I prosecute those I thought were innocent."

Kent earned two associate's degrees, one in law enforcement and one in medical lab technology. His logic was that the degrees would help him find work as either a police officer or forensic investigator. He also hoped that earning a bachelor's degree would help him secure a position as a federal law enforcement officer.

Kent was seeking work as a forensic investigator when he learned of an opening as a probation officer in the adult probation office, which handles felonies and domestic relations cases. He did not get that job, but soon after was offered the position of bailiff.

As Kent says, "I was disappointed at first, but now I'm glad that I'm a bailiff instead of a probation officer. As a bailiff, you are sometimes the judge's ambassador to the community. You have more of a chance to meet both sides."

**Advice from Kent Reeves.** Kent has some sound advice for future bailiffs: "Don't do this job if you are thin-skinned or don't want to work hard. Long hours are not uncommon. If you think that a bailiff job is nine to five, then you should look elsewhere.

"Although most people think that the courts are an arm of the police, we are really the arena that both sides use. A lot of times you get just as much abuse from the police as you do from the defendants. Since we are usually the contact between the police and the courts, when something happens that the police don't like, they usually vent their frustrations on the bailiffs. Also, as bailiffs we are in charge of court security—which sometimes they can't understand. We must take it in stride.

"To prepare yourself when you start out job hunting to be a bailiff, I would suggest classes that would help you understand the legal system in your state and/or community. Bailiffs in jurisdictions our size or smaller are usually hired by the judge. In larger jurisdictions, they are probably hired by the chief bailiff or the clerk of the court, so that's the best place to see about openings."

# CHAPTER FIVE

# Paralegals

While lawyers assume ultimate responsibility for legal work, they often delegate many of their tasks to paralegals. In fact, paralegals, also called legal assistants, continue to assume a growing range of tasks in the nation's legal offices and perform many of the same tasks as lawyers. Despite their wide range of responsibilities, however, paralegals are still explicitly prohibited from carrying out duties that are considered to be the practice of law, such as setting legal fees, giving legal advice, and presenting cases in court.

One of a paralegal's most important tasks is helping lawyers prepare for closings, hearings, trials, and corporate meetings. Paralegals investigate the facts of cases and ensure that all relevant information is considered. They also identify appropriate laws, judicial decisions, legal articles, and other materials that are relevant to assigned cases. After they analyze and organize the information, paralegals may prepare written reports that attorneys use in determining how cases should be handled.

When attorneys decide to file lawsuits on behalf of clients, paralegals may help prepare the legal arguments, draft pleadings and motions to be filed with the court, obtain affidavits, and assist attorneys during trials. Paralegals also organize and track files of all important case documents and make them available and easily accessible to attorneys.

In addition to this preparatory work, paralegals perform a number of other vital functions. For example, they help draft contracts, mortgages, separation agreements, and trust instruments. They also may assist in preparing tax returns and planning estates.

Some paralegals coordinate the activities of other law office employees and maintain financial office records.

Paralegals are found in all types of organizations, but most are employed by law firms, corporate legal departments, and various government offices. In these organizations, they can work in many different areas of the law, including litigation, personal injury, corporate law, criminal law, employee benefits, intellectual property, labor law, bankruptcy, immigration, real estate, and family law. As the law has become more complex, paralegals have responded by becoming more specialized. Within specialties, functions often are broken down even further. For example, paralegals specializing in labor law may deal exclusively with employee benefits.

The duties of paralegals differ widely based on the type of organization in which they are employed. Paralegals who work for corporations often assist attorneys with employee contracts, shareholder agreements, stock-option plans, and employee benefit plans. They also may help prepare and file annual financial reports, maintain corporate minute books and record resolutions, and prepare forms to secure loans for the corporation. Paralegals often monitor and review government regulations to ensure that the corporation is aware of new requirements and operates within the law.

In general, paralegals who work in the public sector analyze legal material for internal use, maintain reference files, conduct research for attorneys, and collect and analyze evidence for agency hearings. They may then prepare informative or explanatory material on laws, agency regulations, and agency policy for general use by the agency and the public. Paralegals employed in community legal-service projects help the poor, the aged, and others in need of legal assistance. They file forms, conduct research, prepare documents, and, when authorized by law, may represent clients at administrative hearings.

Paralegals working in small and medium-sized law firms usually perform a variety of duties that require a general knowledge of the law. For example, they may research judicial decisions on improper police arrests or help prepare mortgage contracts. Paralegals employed by large law firms, government agencies, and corporations, however, are more likely to specialize in one aspect of the law.

Computer facility and technical knowledge have become essential to paralegal work. Computer software packages and the Internet are increasingly used to search legal literature stored in computer databases and on CD-ROM. In litigation involving many supporting documents, paralegals may use computer databases to retrieve, organize, and index various materials. Imaging software allows paralegals to scan documents directly into a database, while billing programs help them to track hours billed to clients. Computer software packages also may be used to perform tax computations and explore the consequences of possible tax strategies for clients.

In summary, the duties of a paralegal are as follows:

1. Take direct responsibility from the attorney for a variety of functions, such as drafting motions, interrogatories to the opposing side, complaints, and correspondence.
2. Regularly deal directly with clients and opposing counsel.
3. At the discretion of the attorney, be autonomous in some areas and have authority when dealing with opposing counsel.
4. Do legal research.
5. Prepare flow charts in complex cases.
6. Prepare cases for trial, e.g., trial binders and evaluation of evidence.
7. Employ computer technology in many aspects of the work.

# Working Conditions

Paralegals employed by corporations and government usually work a standard forty-hour week. Although most paralegals work year-round, some are temporarily employed during busy times of the year, then released when the workload diminishes. Paralegals who work for law firms sometimes work very long hours when they are under pressure to meet deadlines. Some law firms reward such loyalty with bonuses and additional time off.

Paralegals handle many routine assignments, particularly when they are inexperienced. As they gain experience, paralegals usually assume more varied tasks with additional responsibility. Paralegals do most of their work at desks in offices and law libraries. Occasionally, they travel to gather information and perform other duties.

## Training for Paralegals

Some employers train paralegals on the job, hiring college graduates with no legal experience or promoting experienced legal secretaries. Other entrants have experience in a technical field that is useful to law firms, such as a background in tax preparation for tax and estate practice, criminal justice, or nursing or health administration for personal injury practice. Most paralegals, however, pursue professional training of some type.

Formal paralegal training programs are offered by an estimated six hundred colleges and universities, law schools, and proprietary schools. Approximately 250 paralegal programs are approved by the American Bar Association (ABA). Although this approval is neither required nor sought by many programs, graduation from an ABA-approved program often enhances one's employment opportunities. The requirements for admission to these programs vary. Some programs require certain college courses or a bachelor's degree; others accept high school graduates or those with legal experience, and a few require standardized tests and personal interviews.

Options for paralegal training include two-year associate's degree programs, four-year bachelor's degree programs, and certificate programs that can take only a few months to complete.

Most certificate programs provide intensive paralegal training for individuals who already hold college degrees, while associate's and bachelor's degree programs usually combine paralegal training with courses in other academic subjects.

The quality of paralegal training programs varies; the better programs usually include job placement. Programs increasingly include courses introducing students to the legal applications of computers, including how to perform legal research using the Internet. Many paralegal training programs include an internship in which students gain practical experience by working for several months in a private law firm, office of a public defender or attorney general, bank, corporate legal department, legal-aid organization, or government agency. Experience gained in internships is an asset when seeking a job after graduation. Prospective students should examine the experiences of recent graduates before enrolling in those programs.

Although most employers do not require certification, earning a voluntary certificate from a professional society may offer advantages in the labor market. The National Association of Legal Assistants, for example, has established standards for certification requiring various combinations of education and experience. Paralegals who meet these standards are eligible to take a two-day examination, given three times each year at several regional testing centers. Those who pass this examination may use the designation Certified Legal Assistant (CLA). In addition, the Paralegal Advanced Competency Exam, established in 1996 and administered through the National Federation of Paralegal Associations, offers professional recognition to paralegals with a bachelor's degree and at least two years of experience. Those who pass this examination may use the designation Registered Paralegal (RP).

Paralegals must be able to document and present their findings and opinions to their supervising attorney. They need to understand legal terminology and have good research and investigative skills. Familiarity with the operation and applications of computers in legal research and litigation support also is increasingly important. Paralegals should stay informed of new developments in the laws that affect their area of practice. Participation in continuing legal education seminars allows paralegals to maintain and expand their legal knowledge.

Because paralegals frequently deal with the public, they should be courteous and uphold the ethical standards of the legal profession. The National Association of Legal Assistants, the National Federation of Paralegal Associations, and a few states have established ethical guidelines for paralegals to follow.

Paralegals usually are given more responsibilities and less supervision as they gain work experience. Experienced paralegals who work in large law firms, corporate legal departments, and government agencies may supervise and delegate assignments to other paralegals and clerical staff.

Advancement opportunities also include promotion to managerial and other law-related positions within the firm or corporate legal department. However, some paralegals find it easier to move to another law firm when seeking increased responsibility or advancement.

## Employment Figures

Paralegals and legal assistants held about two hundred thousand jobs in 2002. Private law firms employed seven out of ten paralegals and legal assistants; most of the remainder worked for corporate legal departments and various levels of government. Within the federal government, the U.S. Department of Justice is the largest employer, followed by the Social Security Administration and the U.S. Department of Treasury. A small number of paralegals own their own businesses and work as freelance legal assistants, contracting their services to attorneys or corporate legal departments.

# Job Outlook

Employment for paralegals and legal assistants is projected to grow faster than the average for all occupations through 2012. Some employment growth stems from law firms and other employers with legal staffs increasingly hiring paralegals to lower overhead costs and increase the availability and efficiency of legal services.

The majority of job openings for paralegals in the future will be new jobs created by employment growth, but additional job openings will arise as people leave the occupation. Despite projections of fast employment growth, competition for jobs should continue as many people seek to enter this profession; however, highly skilled, formally trained paralegals have excellent employment potential.

Private law firms will continue to be the largest employers of paralegals, but a growing number of other organizations, such as corporate legal departments, insurance companies, real estate and title insurance firms, and banks, hire paralegals. Corporations, in particular, are boosting their in-house legal departments to cut overall costs.

Demand for paralegals also is expected to grow as an increasing population requires legal services, especially in areas such as intellectual property, criminal law, health care, environmental law, elder issues, and international law. The growth of prepaid legal plans also should contribute to the demand for legal services.

Paralegal employment is expected to increase as organizations presently employing paralegals assign them a growing range of tasks and as paralegals are increasingly employed in small and medium-sized establishments. A growing number of experienced paralegals are expected to establish their own businesses.

Job opportunities for paralegals should expand in the public sector as well. Community legal-service programs, which provide assistance to the poor, aged, minorities, and middle-income families, will employ additional paralegals to minimize expenses and serve the most people. Federal, state, and local government agencies, consumer organizations, and the courts also should continue to hire paralegals in increasing numbers.

To a limited extent, paralegal jobs are affected by the business cycle. During recessions, demand declines for some discretionary legal services, such as planning estates, drafting wills, and handling real estate transactions. Corporations are less inclined to initiate certain types of litigation when falling sales and profits lead to fiscal belt tightening. As a result, full-time paralegals employed in offices adversely affected by a recession may be laid off or have their work hours reduced.

On the other hand, during recessions, corporations and individuals are more likely to face other problems that require legal assistance, such as bankruptcies, foreclosures, and divorces. Paralegals, who provide many of the same legal services as lawyers at a lower cost, tend to fare relatively better in difficult economic conditions.

## Earnings

Earnings of paralegals and legal assistants vary greatly. Salaries depend on education, training, experience, type and size of employer, and geographic location of the job. In general, paralegals who work for large law firms or in large metropolitan areas earn more than those who work for smaller firms or in less-populated regions. In addition to a salary, many paralegals receive bonuses.

In 2002, full-time paralegals and legal assistants earned median annual salaries, including bonuses, of $37,950. The middle 50 percent earned between $30,020 and $48,760. The highest-paid 10 percent earned more than $61,150, while the lowest 10 percent earned less than $24,470. Median annual earnings in the industries employing the largest numbers of paralegals in 2002 were as follows:

| | |
|---|---|
| Federal government | $53,770 |
| Legal services | $36,780 |
| Local government | $36,030 |
| State government | $34,750 |

# What It's Really Like

## Barbara Grace Lake, Legal Assistant

Barbara Grace Lake worked in the legal field for twenty years. She worked for small plaintiff personal injury firms and large insurance defense firms.

Barbara's typical day was quite busy. Her agenda might include answering interrogatories, filing a complaint, and compiling the records for a settlement negotiation, among other duties. Any of these tasks could involve follow-up telephone calls with clients, or even visits to clients' homes to secure their statements.

The daily mail brought additional work, such as answers to complaints and depositions. Barbara would then work according to what needed to be done in that day.

One part of the job that required strict attention was filing complaints with the court. For example, personal injury cases carry a one-year statute of limitations. Therefore, if someone is injured on March 1, his complaint must be filed on or before the following March 1. Failure to file in a timely manner means the client has lost the right to sue and can then sue the attorney for malpractice. As Barbara says, "Almost any other deadline can be negotiated, but not this one."

Barbara is candid about her job: "The work is tense and intense. Every day brought a new set of deadlines. Every day was a juggling act. I'd be working on one document, trying to get it out of the way so it could get down to court, but before I could finish that, another document had to be completed because the attorney signing it was leaving at 11 A.M. for a deposition and wouldn't be back in time for it to be signed and in today's mail. Then I'd hurry to finish the next because a client was coming in, and it just went on and on.

"A legal assistant hits the door at a run and, after working a ten- or eleven-hour day, doesn't stop running until he or she is in the car going home. Half the time I had to take work home to finish and bring in first thing in the morning. My average work week was fifty to seventy hours."

Barbara talks about the aspects of the job that she both liked and disliked:

"Some of my work was really quite dull: research, deposition indices in cases going to trial, flow charts, and dramatis personae charts. But all of it was under time pressure. That's the nature of the business.

"On the plus side was the satisfaction in doing a difficult job ably and well. Also, from receptionists to attorneys, one's coworkers are generally brighter than the average found in, for instance, a large insurance office or state agency.

"By the same token, bright people under intense pressure can sometimes be downright churlish. The constant pressure, then, I believe, is a major drawback. Then, too, unless a legal assistant wants to go to law school, it's a dead end job. Legal assistants are already at the top of their field, and there is nowhere to go *up*."

**How Barbara Grace Lake Got Started.** Barbara completed two years of undergraduate study at American River College in Sacramento, California. While today most legal assistants have some formal training for the job, Barbara did not.

"In my case, I went to work in a very small plaintiff personal injury firm and was trained by the attorneys. I still maintain that the best training in the world for a legal assistant is to work for three lazy attorneys who are more than happy to let him or her do the work. I was hired because I was able to write.

"Just prior to looking for work in the legal field, I was a senior clerk in charge of a branch office of the Department of Rehabilitation in Reseda, California. I was called for jury duty. I was so intrigued by the workings of the law during jury duty—by the attorneys each playing their hands to their client's best advantage, by the judge—that I felt I had to get into this field of work."

**Advice from Barbara Grace Lake.** Barbara offers this advice about succeeding in a career as a legal assistant: "By all means take whatever courses are offered in your area to help prepare you for the job ahead. Always be scrupulously honest. By that I mean direct. If an attorney asks if you know something and you don't, don't hedge. Answer honestly, 'I do not know, but give me ten minutes and I'll have an answer for you,' and then get that answer.

"Join whatever legal assistant or paralegal organization is in your area and develop contacts in other law offices. As long as you are not working at opposite ends of a court case, some of your best help is going to come from more-experienced legal assistants. Don't try to go it alone. All you will get for your pains is an ulcer."

# CHAPTER SIX

# Legal Secretaries

egal secretaries are responsible for a variety of administrative and clerical duties necessary to run an organization efficiently. They serve as information managers, plan and schedule meetings and appointments, organize and maintain paper and electronic files, manage projects, conduct research, and provide information by telephone, postal mail, and e-mail. They also may handle travel arrangements.

More specifically, the duties of legal secretaries generally include the following:

1. Prepare documents, correspondence, pleadings, and other materials at the direction of the legal assistant, paralegal, or attorney, employing computer skills and specialized knowledge.
2. Be informed about court filing rules and fees and responsible for the proper filing of documents.
3. Keep a legal calendar for attorneys.
4. Proofread documents for factual, grammatical, or typographical errors.
5. Maintain files in good order.
6. Handle phones and e-mail.

The legal secretary's job in most large firms, then, is one of production at the direction of attorneys and legal assistants. Except in matters of obvious routine and the use of company formats, the legal secretary does not independently generate work. In some small firms, though, jobs and job titles are often blurred, with the assistant or paralegal on occasion doing the work of a secretary and the secretary at times doing the work of an assistant. (For more information on paralegals or legal assistants, see Chapter 5.)

Legal secretaries use personal computers to create spreadsheets, compose correspondence, manage databases, and create presentations, reports, and documents by using desktop-publishing software and digital graphics. Legal secretaries also prepare correspondence and legal papers, such as summonses, complaints, motions, responses, and subpoenas, under the supervision of an attorney or paralegal. They also may review legal journals and assist in other ways with legal research; for example, they may verify quotes and citations in legal briefs.

## Working Conditions

Secretarial jobs often involve sitting for long periods. If secretaries spend a lot of time typing, particularly at a monitor, they may encounter problems such as eyestrain, stress, or carpal tunnel syndrome, which is caused by the repetitive motions used in typing.

Office work can lend itself to alternative or flexible working arrangements, such as part-time work or telecommuting, especially if the job requires extensive computer use. About one secretary in six overall works part-time, and many others work in temporary positions. A few participate in job-sharing arrangements in which two people divide responsibility for a single job. The majority of secretaries, however, are full-time employees who work a standard forty-hour week.

## Training for Legal Secretaries

High school graduates who have basic office skills may qualify for entry-level secretarial positions. However, employers increasingly require extensive knowledge of software applications, such as for word processing, spreadsheets, and database management. Secretaries and administrative assistants should be proficient in keyboarding and good at spelling, punctuation, grammar, and oral communication.

Secretaries and administrative assistants must be tactful in their dealings with people, so employers also look for good customer service and interpersonal skills. Discretion, good judgment, organizational or management ability, initiative, and the ability to work independently are especially important for higher-level administrative positions.

As office automation continues to evolve, retraining and continuing education will remain an integral part of secretarial jobs. Changes in the office environment have increased the demand for secretaries and administrative assistants who are adaptable and versatile. Secretaries may have to attend classes or participate in online education in order to learn how to operate new office technologies, such as information storage systems, scanners, the Internet, or updated software packages. They may also get involved in selecting and maintaining equipment.

Secretarial skills can be acquired in a number of ways. Training ranges from high school vocational education programs that teach office skills and keyboarding to one- and two-year programs in office administration offered by business schools, vocational-technical institutes, and community colleges. Many temporary placement agencies also provide formal training in computer and office skills. However, many skills tend to be acquired through on-the-job instruction by other employees or by equipment and software vendors. Specialized training programs are available for students planning to become legal secretaries. Bachelor's degrees and professional certifications are becoming increasingly important as business continues to become more global.

Testing and certification for proficiency in entry-level office skills is available through the International Association of Administrative Professionals, National Association of Legal Secretaries

(NALS), and Legal Secretaries International. As secretaries and administrative assistants gain experience, they can earn several designations, including Certified Professional Secretary (CPS) or Certified Administrative Professional (CAP), both of which can be earned by meeting experience and/or educational requirements and passing an examination.

Those with one year of experience in the legal field, or who have completed an approved training course and who want to be certified as a legal support professional, can acquire the Accredited Legal Secretary (ALS) designation through a test administered by NALS.

NALS offers two additional credentials: the Professional Legal Secretary (PLS) designation, considered an advanced certification for legal support professionals, and a designation for proficiency as a paralegal. Legal Secretaries International confers the Certified Legal Secretary Specialist (CLSS) designation in areas such as intellectual property, criminal law, civil litigation, probate, and business law to those who have five years of law-related experience and pass an examination. In some instances, certain requirements may be waived.

## Employment Figures

Secretaries and administrative assistants held about 4.1 million jobs in 2002, making this among the largest occupations in the U.S. economy. The following tabulation shows the distribution of employment by secretarial specialty.

| | |
|---|---|
| Secretaries (excluding legal, medical, and executive) | 1,975,000 |
| Executive secretaries and administrative assistants | 1,526,000 |
| Medical secretaries | 339,000 |
| Legal secretaries | 264,000 |

Secretaries are employed in organizations of every type. Approximately nine out of ten secretaries and administrative assistants are employed in service-providing industries; most of the rest work in manufacturing or construction.

## Job Outlook

Overall employment of secretaries and administrative assistants is expected to grow more slowly than the average for all occupations through 2012. In addition to those resulting from growth, numerous job openings will result each year from the need to replace workers who transfer to other occupations or leave this very large occupation for other reasons. Opportunities should be best for experienced secretaries who have extensive knowledge of software applications.

Projected employment of secretaries will vary by occupational specialty. Rapidly growing industries—such as administrative and support services; health care and social assistance; private educational services; and professional, scientific, and technical services—will continue to generate most new job opportunities.

Employment growth in the health care, social assistance, and legal services industries should lead to average growth for medical and legal secretaries. Employment of executive secretaries and administrative assistants is projected to grow more slowly than the average for all occupations. A decline in employment is expected for all other secretaries, except legal, medical, or executive.

Increasing office automation and organizational restructuring will continue to make secretaries and administrative assistants more productive in coming years. Personal computers, e-mail, scanners, and voice message systems will allow secretaries to accomplish more in the same amount of time. The use of automated equipment is also changing the distribution of work in many offices. In some cases, such traditional secretarial duties as keyboarding, filing, photocopying, and bookkeeping are being assigned to workers in other units or departments. Professionals and managers increasingly handle the majority of their own word processing and data entry rather than submit the work to secretaries and other support staff.

In some law firms, paralegals are assuming some tasks formerly done by secretaries. As other workers assume more of their secretarial work, there is a trend in many offices away from the traditional arrangement of one secretary per manager; instead, secretaries and administrative assistants increasingly support entire systems, departments, or units. This approach often means that secretaries and administrative assistants assume added responsibilities and are seen as valuable members of a team, but it also contributes to the projected decline in the overall number of secretaries and administrative assistants.

Developments in office technology are certain to continue, and they will bring about further changes in the work of legal secretaries and administrative assistants. However, many secretarial and administrative duties are of a personal, interactive nature and, therefore, not easily automated. Responsibilities such as planning conferences, working with clients, and instructing staff require tact and communication skills. Because technology cannot substitute for these personal skills, secretaries and administrative assistants will continue to play a key role in most organizations.

## What It's Really Like

### Jennifer Franks, Legal Secretary

Jennifer Franks is a legal secretary and an assistant estate administrator in a general-practice law firm that specializes in family law, estate planning, estate administration, real-estate transactions, and assorted other areas. She works in Delaware County, Pennsylvania.

Most of Jennifer's days are spent translating dictation into letters to clients, other attorneys, and judges. Normally a legal secretary would handle the incoming mail, but Jennifer's boss prefers to open his own mail. Jennifer occasionally answers the telephones when the receptionist is on a break. Calls for Jennifer's boss are routed directly to him; however, if he is on another call, she handles it. "I find out if I can answer a question or be of any assistance or just take a message. Oftentimes the caller just needs some information that I can retrieve from a file and pass along, but knowing what's confidential and what isn't is important. If I have any doubts, I let the attorney handle it. So far, I've been lucky.

"I also make appointments for the attorney I work for, although, again, he likes to handle this kind of thing himself."

Jennifer works from nine to five, Monday through Friday. She generally enjoys her job: "Our workplace is full of camaraderie and laughter. It's like a second family. Sometimes we have fights and get on each other's nerves, but for the most part we know that we rely heavily on each other for mutual support. It's a really good feeling to know that the attorneys feel you are competent and that they appreciate your hard work. Being an assistant is extremely rewarding even if you're not making all the decisions."

Jennifer describes the downside of her job: "I suppose the part I like least about my job is the stigma that is attached to it. People seem to think that because you're a secretary you can't do anything else (just wait until they need one!). As far as the actual daily work goes, the least favorite part of the job is having to be at the beck and call of someone else. You report to people higher up, and they have control of what you do with your time."

**How Jennifer Franks Got Started.** Jennifer has a bachelor's degree in elementary education. Soon after graduation, she was offered a job as a legal secretary by the mother of a friend who had her own legal practice. Jennifer took the job because, as she says, "I was fairly certain that after all the years of college for a degree in elementary education, I really didn't want to teach—not yet, anyway. I had never worked as a legal secretary before and had no idea what I was doing."

Jennifer's friend gave her some initial training, but she was still nervous. "She showed me around the office on a Saturday afternoon, using words I had never heard before, such as 'pleadings.' I was swimming in fear that I would botch everything. I had never even used the word processing program before. Every last detail was new to me. The only thing I had going for me was that I knew I was capable of doing the job."

Within two weeks Jennifer knew the job well, including the legal terminology and the word processing program. Less than a year later, however, the business closed. A year after that, Jennifer found a job through a headhunter service.

Jennifer says, "I completed a two-week probationary period during which I got to know the attorneys in the firm and they got to know me. By the end of the two weeks, I had proved to them that I was more than capable of handling the responsibility, knew the field, knew the word processing programs, and was easy to get along with. I've been here for three years now."

**Advice from Jennifer Franks.** Jennifer has some words of advice for anyone interested in working as a legal secretary: "It is extremely important to be organized. I find that I get the most accomplished if I've a set place for everything and can get my hands on it easily and quickly. The other most important trait is to be confident under pressure.

"It's also extremely important to be able to prioritize. Attorneys often depend on their secretaries to be able to determine for themselves what will take priority. To do that you must have an understanding of where all the projects are in their completion and what their deadlines are and then be able to make a rational decision about what needs to get done first."

## Gigi Starnes, Legal Secretary

Gigi Starnes worked as a legal secretary for a one-lawyer firm. She graduated from a business college with a degree as an executive secretary. Gigi worked at the law firm from 8:00 A.M. to 5:30 P.M. She opened the office, checked messages, and sorted and opened the mail. Gigi also handled the firm's banking deposits and paid the bills. A large part of her day was spent typing, transcribing tapes her boss had dictated.

Gigi kept her employer apprised of his court schedule and appointments, and she maintained a file on each client. She also became a notary public and witnessed a variety of document signings.

Gigi's responsibilities also included filing papers at the court-house, picking up and delivering papers, and making sure dates were correct and that procedures were followed. She also main-tained the attorney's law library, filing new additions to each vol-ume, keeping all subscriptions in an orderly manner and all volumes in their proper places. "This was tedious work, but I learned a lot. The more I worked with the library, the more quickly I could find needed information."

Since the entire staff consisted of only Gigi and her boss, the office door was kept locked at all times. "Being responsible for knowing when to unlock the door to someone was quite a dis-turbing part of my job. I didn't know all the clients, nor did I know the normal routine for service and delivery personnel. My first day on the job, the bell rang and my boss asked me who was there. When I told him, he ran over to my desk and pointed to the bot-tom drawer. I opened it and saw a handgun. 'You do know how to shoot, don't you?' he asked. When I answered in the affirmative, he opened the door and had a rather nasty verbal exchange with an unhappy client. My boss had been a policeman in earlier days and had put himself through law school. His philosophy was that every person deserved a fair trial, and he often took clients other lawyers wouldn't represent."

In summary, Gigi says, "There was more work in one day than I could handle. No two days were ever the same; each brought a new problem to be solved, a new client to serve, a new task to learn. While this is what made the job interesting and challenging, it's also what made it exhausting and stressful."

**How Gigi Starnes Got Started.** Gigi had worked as a secretary, file supervisor, and radio operator until she stopped to raise her children. When she decided to reenter the job market after her children were grown, she attended community college in preparation for a new job.

Gigi applied for several secretarial jobs for which she was qualified, but no offers were forthcoming. She says, "It finally dawned on me that my age was definitely a factor. (Even though we all know that's not supposed to happen, the reality is, it does.) So I branched out and began applying for a variety of jobs, some of which I was not qualified for. And that is how I became a legal secretary."

Following a lengthy interview, Gigi was offered a job at a legal office. She describes the beginning of that job: "The interview was informal and the work sounded interesting and challenging. I was questioned not only about my skills but was also asked to respond to various 'what-would-you-do-if' questions."

Gigi was hired and began working the next day, with almost no training in the office's procedures. Her responsibilities in this position included transcribing tapes, answering the telephone and handling messages, filing, sorting mail, and accounting.

**Advice from Gigi Starnes.** Her experience in the field has led Gigi Starnes to offer some advice about her profession:

"If you're considering becoming a legal secretary, there are some things you can do to prepare yourself. First of all, learn the lingo. Every profession has its own terminology, and you'll be miles ahead if you already know what to listen for. Have at your side an instant word guide for law and a copy of the *Legal Secretary's Complete Handbook*.

"Be aware that part of your job is hearing sensitive and confidential information and that you have a responsibility to keep it to yourself. You will carry tremendous responsibility on your shoulders—your attorneys and their clients depend on you.

"The rewards are great. Not only are you well paid, but as a legal secretary, you stand tall in your profession. If you're good at your job, you are held in high esteem by important people and are given as much responsibility as you are willing to assume. While there are routine tasks to perform, the work is never dull—ever-changing problems cross your desk daily."

# CHAPTER SEVEN

# Law Enforcement Officers

For those interested in the enforcement side of the law, there are many avenues to explore, from police officer to FBI agent, from U.S. Customs official to Canadian Mountie. The safety of our cities, towns, borders, waterways, and highways depends on the work of police officers, sheriffs, detectives, and special agents. Particularly in these times of increased national security, the field of law enforcement is more important than ever as the government strives to maintain public safety.

## Jobs for Law Enforcement Officers

In this chapter we will look at various law enforcement career options, considering the job requirements, nature of the work, availability of positions, and salaries.

### State and Local Police

**Police Officers.** Police work can vary from one location to another, particularly when comparing small towns and large cities. Two common denominators, however, are the mission of each police department to protect its citizens and the dedication of each officer to uphold the law and to investigate and prevent crime. Regardless of the size of the town or the number of officers on the force, police departments nationwide seek highly qualified individuals who meet strict standards of employment.

People depend on police officers to protect their lives and property. In most jurisdictions, officers are expected to exercise authority when necessary, whether on or off duty. Police departments are usually organized into geographic districts, with uniformed officers assigned to patrol specific areas. Some officers specialize in specific fields, such as chemical analysis, firearms instruction, or fingerprint identification. Others work with special units, such as horseback, harbor patrol, or canine corps.

**Detectives.** Detectives are plainclothes investigators who gather facts and collect evidence for criminal cases. They conduct interviews, examine records, observe the activities of suspects, and participate in raids or arrests. Detectives usually specialize in a specific area of crime, such as homicide or fraud. In most instances they are assigned cases on a rotating basis and work on them until an arrest and conviction occurs or the case is dropped.

**Sheriffs and Deputy Sheriffs.** Sheriffs enforce the law on the county level. They are usually elected to their positions and perform duties similar to those of a local or county police chief. Sheriffs' departments are normally small, most with fewer than twenty-five sworn officers. A deputy sheriff in a larger department has duties similar to those of officers who work in urban police departments.

**State Police Officers.** State police officers (or state troopers) provide law enforcement statewide in addition to patrolling highways to enforce motor vehicle and traffic laws. They often respond to accident scenes, directing traffic, giving first aid, and calling for emergency equipment. Every state except Hawaii has a state police department.

## Federal Agents

In addition to local and state police departments, the federal government plays a major role in law enforcement. Several agencies, most under the purview of the Department of Justice, employ special agents to carry out the federal government's law enforcement needs. Here is a look at the United States federal agencies that are involved in law enforcement.

**Federal Bureau of Investigation (FBI).** FBI agents are the government's principal investigators, enforcing over 260 statutes and conducting sensitive national-security investigations. Agents conduct surveillance, monitor court-authorized wiretaps, investigate white-collar crime, and collect evidence of espionage.

The FBI investigates organized crime, public corruption, fraud against the government, copyright infringement, civil rights violations, bank robberies, extortion, kidnapping, air piracy, terrorism, interstate criminal activities, drug trafficking, and other violations of federal statutes. The FBI also works with other federal, state, and local law enforcement agencies to investigate matters of joint interest and to train law enforcement officers from around the world.

**U.S. Drug Enforcement Administration (DEA).** DEA agents enforce laws relating to illegal drugs. The DEA is the lead agency for domestic enforcement of federal drug laws, as well as having sole responsibility for coordinating and pursuing U.S. drug investigations abroad. Agents conduct surveillance and investigations, infiltrate drug trafficking organizations, confiscate illegal drugs, arrest criminals, conduct money-laundering investigations, and testify in criminal court cases.

**U.S. Marshals and Deputy Marshals.** These agents protect the federal courts. Their duties include protecting the federal judiciary, transporting federal prisoners, managing seized assets, and protecting federal witnesses. Federal marshals have the widest jurisdiction of any federal agency and are involved to an extent in almost all federal law enforcement efforts. U.S. Marshals also pursue and arrest federal fugitives.

**U.S. Customs Service.** Customs agents investigate cases of narcotics smuggling, money laundering, child pornography, customs fraud, and enforcement of the Arms Export Control Act. Now under the direction of the Department of Homeland Security, customs agents conduct interviews and serve on joint task forces with other agencies. Investigations can involve the development and use of informants, physical and electronic surveillance, and examination of records from importers and exporters, banks, couriers, and manufacturers.

**U.S. Secret Service.** Also under the oversight of the Department of Homeland Security, Secret Service special agents protect the president, vice president, and their immediate families; presidential candidates; former presidents; and foreign dignitaries visiting the United States. Secret Service agents also investigate counterfeiting, forgery of government checks or bonds, and fraudulent use of credit cards.

**Bureau of Alcohol, Tobacco, Firearms, and Explosives (ATF).** The Department of the Treasury employs ATF agents to enforce and investigate violations of federal firearms and explosives laws, as well as federal alcohol and tobacco tax regulations. These agents might investigate suspected illegal sales of guns or the underpayment of taxes by a liquor or cigarette manufacturer.

**Bureau of Diplomatic Security.** Under direction of the Department of State, special agents from this bureau are engaged in the battle against terrorism. Overseas, they advise ambassadors on all security matters and manage a complex range of security programs designed to protect personnel, facilities, and information. In the United States, they investigate passport and visa fraud, conduct personnel security investigations, issue security clearances, and protect the secretary of state and a number of foreign dignitaries. They also train civilian police and administer a reward program for counter-terrorism efforts.

Several other federal agencies employ police and special agents with sworn arrest powers and the authority to carry firearms. These agencies include the U.S. Postal Service, the Bureau of Indian Affairs, the U.S. Forest Service, the National Park Service, and Federal Air Marshals. Other police agencies have evolved from the need for security for agency property and personnel. The largest such agency is the General Services Administration's Federal Protective Service, which provides security for federal workers, buildings, and property.

## Working Conditions

The work of law enforcement can be very dangerous and stressful. In addition to the obvious dangers of confrontations with criminals, officers need to be constantly alert and ready to deal appropriately with a number of other threatening situations. Many law enforcement officers witness death and suffering resulting from accidents and criminal behavior. A career in law enforcement may take a toll on officers' private lives.

Uniformed officers, detectives, agents, and inspectors are usually scheduled to work forty-hour weeks, but paid overtime is common. Shift work is necessary because protection must be provided around the clock. Junior officers frequently work weekends, holidays, and nights. Police officers and detectives are required to work at any time their services are needed and may work long hours during investigations. In most jurisdictions, whether on or off duty, officers are expected to be armed and to exercise their arrest authority whenever necessary.

The jobs of some federal agents, such as U.S. Secret Service and DEA special agents, require extensive travel, often on very short notice. They may relocate a number of times over the course of their careers. Some special agents—U.S. Border Patrol agents, for example—work outdoors in rugged terrain for long periods and in all kinds of weather.

# Training for Law Enforcement Officers

## State and Local Police

In most cities and states, civil service regulations determine the appointment of police officers. In general, candidates must be U.S. citizens and fall within a specified age range (usually between twenty and thirty-five years of age). Many large police departments require that applicants complete up to sixty college credits by the time of appointment. After passing a written exam, applicants must meet rigorous physical and personal qualifications, including extensive character investigation and psychological testing. Physical ability tests screen for strength, agility, vision, and hearing requirements.

Upon successful completion of all requirements, officers enter a training academy, usually for twelve to fourteen weeks. Training includes classroom instruction in constitutional law and civil rights, state and local laws, and accident investigation. Recruits are also trained in the use of firearms, traffic control, self-defense, first aid, and emergency response.

Police officers usually become eligible for promotion after a probationary period ranging from six months to three years. In a large department, promotion may enable an officer to become a detective or to specialize in one type of work, such as working with juveniles. Promotions within the uniformed ranks to grades such as sergeant, lieutenant, and captain are usually made according to an officer's position on a promotion list, which is determined by scores on written examinations and job performance.

## Federal Agents

To be considered for appointment as an FBI agent, an applicant must be either a graduate of an accredited law school or a college graduate with a major in accounting, fluency in a foreign language, or three years of related full-time work experience. All new agents undergo sixteen weeks of training at the FBI academy on the U.S. Marine Corps base in Quantico, Virginia.

An applicant for a special-agent job with the U.S. Secret Service or the Bureau of Alcohol, Tobacco, Firearms, and Explosives must have a bachelor's degree or a minimum of three years' related work experience. Prospective special agents undergo ten weeks of initial criminal investigation training at the Federal Law Enforcement Training Center in Glynco, Georgia, and another seventeen weeks of specialized training with their particular agencies.

An applicant for a special-agent job with the U.S. Drug Enforcement Administration (DEA) must have a college degree and either one year of experience conducting criminal investigations, one year of graduate school, or have achieved at least a 2.95 grade point average while in college. DEA special agents undergo fourteen weeks of specialized training at the FBI Academy in Quantico, Virginia.

U.S. Border Patrol agents must be U.S. citizens, be younger than thirty-seven years of age at the time of appointment, possess a valid driver's license, and pass a three-part examination on reasoning and language skills. A bachelor's degree or previous work experience that demonstrates the ability to handle stressful situations, make decisions, and take charge is required for a position as a Border Patrol agent. Applicants may qualify through a combination of education and work experience.

Postal inspectors must have a bachelor's degree and one year of related work experience. It is desirable that they have one of several professional certifications, such as that of certified public accountant. They also must pass a background suitability investigation, meet certain health requirements, undergo a drug screening test, possess a valid state driver's license, and be a U.S. citizen between twenty-one and thirty-six years of age when hired.

Law enforcement agencies are encouraging applicants to take postsecondary school training in law enforcement–related subjects. Many entry-level applicants for police jobs have completed some formal postsecondary education, and a significant number are college graduates. Many junior colleges, colleges, and universities offer programs in law enforcement or administration of justice.

Other courses helpful in preparing for a career in law enforcement include accounting, finance, electrical engineering, computer science, and foreign languages. Physical education and sports are helpful in developing the competitiveness, stamina, and agility needed for many law enforcement positions. Knowledge of a foreign language is an asset in many federal agencies as well as urban departments.

Continuing training helps police officers, detectives, and special agents improve their job performance. Through police department academies, regional centers for public safety employees, and federal agency training centers, instructors provide annual training in self-defense tactics, firearms, use-of-force policies, sensitivity and communications skills, crowd-control techniques, relevant legal developments, and advances in law enforcement equipment. Many agencies pay all or part of the tuition for officers to work toward degrees in criminal justice, police science, administration of justice, or public administration, and many agencies pay higher salaries to those who earn such a degree.

## The Ride of Your Life

If you are willing to sign an agreement that the police department will be held harmless in case of any "incidents," you could find yourself riding shotgun in a police car. Many police departments across the country allow what are called observer rides or ridealongs. Interested participants spend an entire shift with an on-duty law enforcement officer.

As an observer, you might spend a routine shift in a car with little activity. On the other hand, you might find yourself riding along as the officer responds to any variety of crimes. Robberies, domestic disputes, drug busts, and even homicide investigations are all possibilities.

All sorts of people take advantage of observer rides. Law and criminal justice students, writers, career investigators, and private citizens concerned about their communities have all participated in ride-alongs. To arrange an observer ride, contact the public information office of your local police department.

## Employment Figures

Police and detectives held about 840,000 jobs in 2002. About 81 percent worked for local governments. State police agencies employed approximately 11 percent; federal agencies employed about 6 percent. A small proportion worked for educational services, rail transportation, and contract investigation and security services.

According to the U.S. Bureau of Justice statistics, police and detectives employed by local governments primarily worked in cities with more than twenty-five thousand inhabitants. Some cities have very large police forces, while thousands of small communities employ fewer than twenty-five officers each.

## Job Outlook

The opportunity for public service through law enforcement work is attractive to many because the job is challenging and involves much personal responsibility. Furthermore, law enforcement officers in many agencies may retire with a pension after twenty or twenty-five years of service, allowing them to pursue a second career while still in their forties. Because of relatively attractive salaries and benefits, the number of qualified candidates exceeds the number of job openings in federal law enforcement agencies and in most state police departments, resulting in increased hiring standards and selectivity by employers.

Competition should remain keen for higher-paying jobs with state and federal agencies and police departments in more affluent areas. Opportunities will be better in local and special police departments, especially in departments that offer relatively low salaries or in urban communities where the crime rate is relatively high. Applicants with college training in police science, military police experience, or both should have the best opportunities.

Employment of police officers and detectives is expected to grow faster than the average for all occupations through 2012. A more security-conscious society and concern about drug-related crimes should contribute to the increasing demand for police services.

The level of government spending determines the level of employment for police and detectives. The number of job opportunities, therefore, can vary from year to year and from place to place. Layoffs, on the other hand, are rare because most staffing cuts are handled through attrition. Trained law enforcement officers who lose their jobs because of budget cuts usually have little difficulty finding jobs with other agencies. The need to replace workers who retire, transfer to other occupations, or stop working for other reasons will be the source of many job openings.

## Earnings

Police and sheriff's patrol officers had median annual earnings of $42,270 in 2002. The middle 50 percent earned between $32,300 and $53,500. The lowest 10 percent earned less than $25,270, and the highest 10 percent earned more than $65,330. Median annual earnings were $47,090 in state government, $42,020 in local government, and $41,600 in the federal government.

In 2002, median annual earnings of police and detective supervisors were $61,010. The middle 50 percent earned between $47,210 and $74,610. The lowest 10 percent earned less than $36,340, and the highest 10 percent earned more than $90,070. Median annual earnings were $78,230 in the federal government, $64,410 in state government, and $59,830 at the local level.

Median annual earnings of detectives and criminal investigators were $51,410. The middle 50 percent earned between $39,010 and $65,980. The lowest 10 percent earned less than $31,010, and the highest 10 percent earned more than $80,380. Median annual earnings were $66,500 in the federal government, $47,700 in local government, and $46,600 in state government.

Federal law provides special salary rates to federal employees who serve in law enforcement. Additionally, federal special agents and inspectors receive law enforcement availability pay (LEAP)—which equals 25 percent of the agent's grade and step—awarded because of the large amount of overtime that these agents are expected to work.

For example, in 2003 FBI agents entered federal service as GS-10 employees on the pay scale at a base salary of $39,115, yet they earned about $48,890 a year with availability pay. They can advance to the GS-13 grade level in field nonsupervisory assignments at a base salary of $61,251, which is worth $76,560 with availability pay.

For FBI supervisory, management, and executive positions in grades GS-14 and GS-15, the base salary was $72,381 and $85,140 a year, respectively, and equaled $90,480 or $106,430 per year with the addition of availability pay.

Salaries were slightly higher in selected areas where the prevailing local pay level was higher. Because federal agents may be eligible for a special law enforcement benefits package, applicants should ask their recruiters for more information.

According to the International City-County Management Association's annual Police and Fire Personnel, Salaries, and Expenditures Survey, average base annual salary ranges for full-time positions in 2002 were as follows:

| | |
|---|---|
| Police chief | $68,337–$87,037 |
| Deputy chief | $59,790–$75,266 |
| Police captain | $56,499–$70,177 |
| Police lieutenant | $52,446–$63,059 |
| Police sergeant | $46,805–$55,661 |
| Police corporal | $39,899–$49,299 |

Total earnings for local, state, and special police and detectives frequently exceed the stated salary because of payments for overtime, which can be significant. In addition to the common benefits—paid vacation, sick leave, and medical and life insurance—most police and sheriff's departments provide officers with special allowances for uniforms. Because police officers usually are covered by liberal pension plans, many retire at half pay after twenty or twenty-five years of service.

# Law Enforcement in Canada

As in the United States, the Canadian government also maintains several federal agencies whose goal is the protection and security of Canadian citizens. Let's take a look at the major agencies that provide law enforcement services in Canada.

## Canada's Department of Justice

The Department of Justice is the largest single legal organization in Canada, employing more than two thousand lawyers from all over the country. Career opportunities at the Department of Justice include working in criminal, civil, and tax litigation; policy development; human rights law; and international law.

Canada's Department of Justice has over forty-five hundred employees who work at the departmental headquarters in Ottawa and in some thirty other federal departments and agencies. Some employees work in the thirteen regional offices and suboffices across the country, helping the department to respond effectively to regional issues.

Approximately half of the Department of Justice staff is made up of lawyers. The other half are experts in fields such as research, social sciences, and communications, as well as paralegals and support staff.

In order to be considered for a legal officer position within Canada's Department of Justice, a candidate must meet the following criteria: be a member in good standing of the law society of one of the provinces or territories of Canada; be a member of the Chamber of Notaries in the Province of Quebec; or be an articling student whose appointment is conditional upon admission to the bar or Chamber of Notaries.

Applicants should have strong interpersonal skills and should value teamwork and have the capacity to adapt to different situations and work environments. Before an offer of employment can be made, an applicant must receive a reliability/security clearance. This may include fingerprinting and the completion of a Personal History Form.

## Canadian Security Intelligence Service

The Canadian Security Intelligence Service (CSIS) is a federal agency dedicated to protecting the national security interests of Canada. The main objective of the CSIS is to investigate and report on threats to the nation's security. The agency is the government's principal advisor on matters of national security.

The core staff of the CSIS is the Intelligence Officer category. Intelligence officers conduct investigations, perform research, analyze information, and prepare reports on national security–related matters. Applicants should be proficient in both official languages; knowledge of foreign languages and computer literacy are also assets. Candidates for intelligence officer must be Canadian citizens, have a university degree, and be willing to relocate anywhere in Canada, depending on the needs of the service.

Intelligence officers serve an initial probationary period of five years. The starting salary is $39,640, progressing to $63,800 during the probationary period, based on successful completion of training, job performance, and attaining the required experience.

## Canada Customs and Revenue Agency

The Canada Customs and Revenue Agency provides protection at Canada's borders, collects taxes, delivers social and economic benefits on behalf of the federal government, and administers trade agreements. In addition, the Customs and Revenue Agency monitors the movement of people and goods across Canada's land, air, and marine borders; conducts audits for large and small businesses; develops and maintains state-of-the-art information technology; and trains detector dogs and provides other special detection services.

The Customs and Revenue Agency is comprised of various occupational groups, hiring employees for positions such as general services clerk, customs inspector, and real-estate appraiser. Each occupational group has its own salary range, and the basic annual pay rate is determined upon hiring.

## Royal Canadian Mounted Police

In addition to federal agencies, the Royal Canadian Mounted Police (RCMP) provides protection to citizens of Canada. As the Canadian national police service, the RCMP also acts as a provincial and municipal police force, providing a total federal police service to all Canadians.

Applicants to the RCMP must meet the following requirements: be a Canadian citizen; be of good character; be proficient in either of Canada's official languages; have a secondary school diploma or its equivalent from a Canadian school; possess a valid, unrestricted Canadian driver's license; be nineteen years of age at the time of acceptance; pass a written aptitude test; meet rigorous physical and medical requirements; and be willing to relocate anywhere within Canada. In addition, prior to enrollment in cadet training, candidates must obtain certificates in keyboarding or typing and first aid.

Salary for an RCMP constable consists of four levels, and the increments are not granted automatically. Officers must complete certain duties and achieve specific experience before receiving salary increases.

The starting salary for a cadet is $39,535 for the first six months or until completion of the field training program. The level increases to $51,367 after completion of field training and during the first two years of service, to $60,099 for the next twelve months, and to $64,059 after three years.

## What It's Really Like

### Ramesh Nyberg, Homicide Detective

Ramesh Nyberg is a homicide detective with the Metro-Dade Police Department in Miami, Florida. He is a member of the department's cold-case squad.

Ramesh says that, unlike what we see on television, it usually takes more than two detectives to solve a crime. In his experience in homicide, detectives work inside the crime scene while others canvass the neighborhood, literally knocking on every door to ask for information. As he says, "Very often people will see things, hear things, or know things but won't say a word until someone knocks on their door."

For this reason, Ramesh says, "I don't think there's any greater weapon in a policeman's arsenal than his own ears and his ability to listen. In street police work, when you're a uniformed officer, you have to be very aware of what people are doing and saying. You can't take a report from someone without listening to them. For purposes of your own safety, you have to listen carefully to what they're saying, their tone of voice, whether it's rising or falling. I think young officers miss this a lot, but there are things people say and things they won't say that they'll only hint at, whether consciously or subconsciously. They have the potential to tell you a lot of things, but without your asking the proper questions, they won't say anything."

Detectives on the cold-case squad try to solve murders that have long been unresolved. Ramesh says that an advantage to this type of work is that the detectives have more time to devote to each case because their work is not interrupted by a newly committed crime that requires their attention.

Solving the puzzle of a cold case often involves working backward. As Ramesh states: "Very often you start out trying to find the original witnesses, making sure they are still around. If they have all died off, there is no use in going forward. Sometimes rehashing old testimony brings out new things or things that people didn't want to talk about before. So you have to look closely at how the landscape of the people's lives has changed. Like regular homicide, skillful interviewing gives you your best chance."

New technology has helped detectives solve crimes in recent years. Police have access to several databases that help them to locate people, and the centralization of most public records— even billing information—makes it easier to find the required information.

**How Ramesh Nyberg Got Started.** Ramesh's interest in police work began when he was about eighteen. As a college student, he studied with a friend who listened to a police scanner. He became fascinated with police work and signed up for an observer ride with local police. "When I was out there with them and saw what the police did firsthand, how they utilized all their senses, not just their authority, but their intellect, too, it really interested me a lot. Two or three observer rides later, I was pretty much hooked on the idea of police work as a profession."

Ramesh's first job with a police department was in Opalocka, Florida. He attended the police academy for five months of training. After a year, Ramesh moved to the North Miami Police Department and stayed for two years. Wanting more opportunities for advancement, Ramesh moved to Metro-Dade, a county police department, and worked on patrol for three years before becoming a detective.

**Advice from Ramesh Nyberg.** Ramesh stresses that detective work requires a certain type of personality. As he says, "You have to be flexible, tenacious, and have convictions. If you don't, then what are you doing here?"

A police officer or detective must be able to put aside emotions and react appropriately to witnesses and suspects. As Ramesh says, "Police work really involves just hard work and determination, observation, and common sense. . . . And I think people who want to become police officers and do become police officers are special people in many ways, but it's simply a matter of applying yourself and being objective."

# CHAPTER EIGHT

# Investigators

L egal eagles who are interested in getting to the bottom of a case and catching wrongdoers red-handed might be most interested in a career in investigative work. While many of us might think only of private investigators, there are actually several careers within investigative work from which to choose. In this chapter, we will look at three investigative specialties: private investigation, insurance investigation, and arson investigation.

## Private Investigators

Private detectives and investigators provide services to attorneys, government agencies, businesses, and the public. Some of their more common activities include gathering information, tracing debtors, and conducting background investigations. The main job of private investigators and detectives is to obtain information and locate assets or individuals. Some private investigators protect stores and hotels from theft, vandalism, and disorder.

Private detectives and investigators use many means to determine the facts in their cases. To carry out investigations, they may use various types of surveillance or searches. To verify facts, such as an individual's place of employment or income, they may make phone calls or visit a subject's workplace. In other cases, especially those involving missing persons and background checks, investigators often interview people to gather as much information as possible about an individual.

Private investigators and detectives offer a variety of services, such as providing executive, corporate, and celebrity protection; conducting pre-employment verification; and preparing individual background profiles. They provide assistance in civil liability and personal injury cases, insurance claims and fraud, child custody and protection cases, and premarital screening. Increasingly, they investigate individuals to prove or disprove infidelity.

Most detectives and investigators are trained to perform physical surveillance, often for long periods, in a car or van. They may observe a site, such as the home of a subject, from an inconspicuous location. The surveillance continues using still and video cameras, binoculars, or enhanced listening devices until the desired evidence is obtained. They also may perform computer database searches or work with someone who does. Computers allow detectives and investigators to quickly obtain massive amounts of information on individuals' prior arrests, convictions, and civil legal judgments; telephone numbers; motor vehicle registrations; association and club memberships; and many other details.

The duties of private detectives and investigators depend on the needs of their clients. In a case involving a fraudulent workers' compensation claim, for example, an investigator may carry out long-term covert observation of the subject. If the investigator observes the subject performing activities that contradict injuries stated in a workers' compensation claim, the investigator would take video or still photographs to document the activity and report it to the client.

## Types of Private Investigators

Private detectives and investigators often specialize. Those who focus on intellectual property theft, for example, investigate and document acts of piracy, help clients stop the illegal activity, and provide intelligence for prosecution and civil action.

Other investigators specialize in developing financial profiles and making asset searches. They prepare reports that reflect information gathered through interviews, investigation, surveillance, and research, including reviews of public documents. What follows is a summary of some of the areas of private investigation:

- **Legal investigators** specialize in cases involving the courts and are normally employed by law firms or lawyers. They frequently assist in preparing criminal defenses, locating witnesses, serving legal documents, interviewing police and prospective witnesses, and gathering and reviewing evidence. Legal investigators also may collect information on the parties to the litigation, take photographs, testify in court, and assemble evidence and reports for trials.
- **Corporate investigators** conduct internal and external investigations for corporations other than investigative firms. In internal investigations, they may investigate drug use in the workplace, ensure that expense accounts are not abused, or determine whether employees are stealing merchandise or selling information. External investigations typically prevent criminal schemes originating outside the corporation, such as theft of company assets through fraudulent billing of products by suppliers.
- **Financial investigators** may be hired to develop confidential financial profiles of individuals or companies who are prospective parties to large financial transactions. These investigators often are Certified Public Accountants (CPAs) and work closely with investment bankers and accountants. They search for hidden assets in order to recover damages awarded by the court in fraud or theft cases.
- **Store detectives**, also known as **loss-prevention agents**, work for retail stores or hotels. They are responsible for loss control and asset protection, safeguarding the assets of retail stores by apprehending anyone attempting to steal merchandise or destroy store property. They prevent theft by shoplifters, vendor representatives, delivery personnel, and even store employees. Store detectives also conduct periodic inspections of stock areas, dressing rooms, and

restrooms, and they sometimes assist in opening and closing the store. They may prepare loss-prevention and security reports for management and testify in court against persons they apprehend.

- **Hotel detectives** protect guests of the establishment from theft of their belongings and preserve order in hotel restaurants and bars. They also may keep undesirable individuals, such as known thieves, off the premises.

## Working Conditions

Private detectives and investigators often work irregular hours because of the need to conduct surveillance and contact people who are not available during normal working hours. Early morning, evening, weekend, and holiday work is common. Many private detectives and investigators spend their time away from their offices conducting interviews or doing surveillance, but some work in their offices most of the day, conducting computer searches and making phone calls. Those who have their own agencies and hire other investigators may work primarily in an office and have normal business hours.

When working on a case away from the office, the environment might range from plush board rooms to seedy bars. Store and hotel detectives work in the businesses that they protect. Investigators generally work alone, but they sometimes work with others during surveillance or when following a subject in order to avoid detection by the subject.

Sometimes the work involves confrontation, so the job can be stressful and dangerous. Some situations, such as bodyguard assignments for corporate or celebrity clients, call for the investigator to be armed. Detectives and investigators who carry handguns must be licensed by the appropriate authority. In most cases, however, a weapon is not necessary because the purpose of the work is gathering information and not law enforcement or criminal apprehension. Owners of investigative agencies have the added stress of dealing with demanding and often distraught clients.

## Training for Private Investigators

There are no formal education requirements for most private detective and investigator jobs, although many private detectives have college degrees. Most private detectives and investigators have previous experience in other occupations. Some work initially for insurance or collections companies or in the private security industry. Many investigators enter the field after serving in law enforcement, the military, government auditing and investigative positions, or federal intelligence jobs.

Former law enforcement officers, military investigators, and government agents often become private detectives or investigators as a second career because they are frequently able to retire after twenty years of service. Others enter from such diverse fields as finance, accounting, commercial credit, investigative reporting, insurance, and law. These individuals often can apply their prior work experience in a related investigative specialty. A few enter the occupation directly after college graduation, generally with associate's or bachelor's degrees in criminal justice or police science.

Most states and the District of Colombia require private detectives and investigators to be licensed. Licensing requirements vary widely, but convicted felons cannot receive a license in most states and a growing number of states are enacting mandatory training programs for private detectives and investigators.

While some states have few requirements, and six states—Alabama, Alaska, Colorado, Idaho, Mississippi, and South Dakota—have no statewide licensing requirements, others have stringent regulations.

Most employers look for individuals with ingenuity, persistence, and assertiveness. A candidate must not be afraid of confrontation, should communicate well, and should be able to think on his or her feet.

Good interviewing and interrogation skills, usually acquired in earlier careers in law enforcement or other fields, are also important. Because the courts often serve as the ultimate judge of whether an investigation was conducted properly, the investigator must be able to present the facts in a manner that a jury will believe.

Training in subjects such as criminal justice is helpful to aspiring private detectives and investigators. Most corporate investigators must have a bachelor's degree, preferably in a business-related field. Some corporate investigators have master's degrees in business administration or law, while others are certified public accountants. Corporate investigators hired by large companies may receive formal training from their employers on business practices, management structure, and various finance-related topics. The screening process for potential employees typically includes a background check of criminal history.

Some investigators receive certification from a professional organization to demonstrate competency in a field. For example, the National Association of Legal Investigators (NALI) confers the Certified Legal Investigator (CLI) designation to licensed investigators who devote a majority of their practice to negligence or criminal defense investigations. To receive the designation, applicants must satisfy experience, educational, and continuing training requirements and must pass written and oral exams administered by NALI.

Most private detective agencies are small, with little room for advancement. Usually there are no defined ranks or steps, so advancement takes the form of increases in salary and assignment status. Many detectives and investigators work for detective agencies at the beginning of their careers and, after a few years, start their own firms. Corporate and legal investigators may be promoted to supervisor or manager of the security or investigations department.

## Employment Figures

Private detectives and investigators held approximately forty-eight thousand jobs in 2002. About a third were self-employed, including many whose secondary jobs were as self-employed private detectives. Almost a fifth of the jobs were found in investigation and security services, including private detective agencies, while another fifth were in department or other general merchandise stores. The rest worked mostly in state and local government, legal services firms, employment services, insurance carriers, and credit intermediation and related activities, including banks and other depository institutions.

## Job Outlook

Keen competition is expected because private detective and investigator careers attract many qualified people, including relatively young retirees from law enforcement and military careers. Opportunities will be best for entry-level jobs with detective agencies or as part-time store detectives. Those seeking store detective jobs usually have the best prospects with large chains and discount stores.

Employment of private detectives and investigators is expected to grow faster than the average for all occupations through 2012. In addition to growth, replacement of those who retire or leave the occupation for other reasons should create many job openings.

Increased demand for private detectives and investigators will result from fear of crime, increased litigation, and the need to protect confidential information and property of all kinds. More private investigators also will be needed to assist attorneys working on criminal defense and civil litigation. Growing financial activity worldwide will increase the demand for investigators to control internal and external financial losses and to monitor competitors and prevent industrial spying.

## Earnings

Median annual earnings of salaried private detectives and investigators were $29,300 in 2002. The middle 50 percent earned between $21,980 and $41,710. The lowest 10 percent earned less than $17,290, and the highest 10 percent earned more than

$57,370. In 2002, median annual earnings were $29,030 in investigation and security services and $22,250 in department stores.

Earnings of private detectives and investigators vary greatly depending on their employer, specialty, and the geographic area in which they work. According to a study by Abbott, Langer & Associates, security and loss-prevention directors and vice presidents had a median income of $77,500 per year in 2002; investigators, $39,800; and store detectives, $25,000. In addition to typical benefits, most corporate investigators received profit-sharing plans.

## Insurance Investigators

Insurance fraud is often thought of as a victimless crime, one that targets large corporations that can afford to absorb the cost of fraud. In reality, however, we all pay for insurance fraud since companies must raise their rates to cover their losses.

Insurance fraud is a deliberate misrepresentation of facts to an insurance carrier with the intention of defrauding the company of money. This crime can affect workers' compensation, medical, life, and property insurance. There are really no boundaries, either monetary or geographic, to insurance fraud.

Individuals and businesses purchase insurance policies to protect against monetary losses. In the event of a loss, policy holders submit claims, or requests for payment, as compensation for their losses. Investigators work primarily for property and casualty insurance companies, for whom they handle a wide variety of claims for property damage, liability, and bodily injury.

Within an insurance company, investigators work in a special investigative unit and handle claims that the company suspects are fraudulent. Arson cases, false workers' disability claims, staged accidents, and unnecessary medical treatments are some of the cases that investigators might work on.

Investigators usually start with a database search to obtain background information on claimants and witnesses. Investigators can access certain personal information and identify social security numbers, aliases, driver's license numbers, addresses, phone numbers, criminal records, and past claims histories to establish whether a claimant has ever attempted insurance fraud. Then, investigators may visit claimants and witnesses to obtain a recorded statement, take photographs, and inspect facilities. For example, an investigator might visit the office of the doctor of record on an insurance claim to determine whether the dictor is properly licensed. Investigators often consult with legal counsel and can serve as expert witnesses in court cases. Often, insurance investigators also perform surveillance work.

## Working Conditions

Insurance investigators, like private detectives, often work irregular hours because of the need to conduct surveillance and contact people who are not available during normal working hours. Early morning, evening, and weekend work is common.

Some days, investigators spend all day in the office conducting database searches, making telephone calls, and writing reports. Other times, they may be away performing surveillance activities or interviewing witnesses. Sometimes the work can involve confrontation with claimants and others involved in a case, so the job can be stressful and dangerous.

## Training for Insurance Investigators

Training and entry requirements vary widely for claims adjusters, appraisers, examiners, and investigators. Although many in these occupations do not have a college degree, most companies prefer to hire college graduates. No specific college major is recommended, but a variety of backgrounds can serve as a good starting place in this field.

Most insurance companies prefer to hire former law enforcement officers or private investigators as insurance investigators. Many experienced claims adjusters or insurance examiners also become investigators. Most employers look for individuals who are creative thinkers. Investigators should be persistent and willing to be assertive if necessary. They must be able to handle confrontational situations and communicate well with people from a wide variety of backgrounds. They also need interviewing and interrogation skills.

Beginning claims adjusters, appraisers, examiners, and investigators work on small claims under the supervision of an experienced investigator. As they learn more about claims investigation and settlement, they are assigned larger, more complex claims to investigate. Trainees are promoted as they demonstrate competence in handling assignments and as they progress in their training. Claims investigators may rise to supervisor or manager of the investigations department.

Licensing requirements vary by state. Some states have very few requirements, while others require the completion of prelicensing education or a satisfactory score on a licensing exam. Check with your state's insurance department for current licensing requirements.

## Employment Figures

Insurance professionals, consisting of investigators, adjusters, appraisers, and examiners, held about 241,000 jobs in 2002. Of these, more than 14,000 were jobs held by auto damage insurance appraisers. Insurance carriers employed nearly 60 percent of claims adjusters, appraisers, examiners, and investigators; more than 20 percent were employed by insurance agencies, brokerages, and private claims adjusting companies. Approximately 2 percent of all adjusters, appraisers, examiners, and investigators were self-employed.

## Job Outlook

Employment of insurance investigators is expected to grow about as fast as the average for all occupations through 2012. Opportunities will be best for those with a college degree. Numerous job openings also will result from the need to replace workers who transfer to other occupations or leave the labor force.

Despite recent gains in productivity resulting from technological advances, these jobs are not easily automated. Adjusters still are needed to contact policy holders, inspect damaged property, and consult with experts.

Although the number of claims in litigation and the number and complexity of insurance fraud cases are expected to increase over the next decade, demand for insurance investigators is not expected to grow significantly. The use of technology, such as the Internet, which reduces the amount of time it takes to perform background checks, will allow investigators to handle more cases.

Competition for investigator jobs will remain keen because the occupation attracts many qualified people, including retirees from law enforcement and military careers, as well as experienced claims adjusters and examiners who choose to obtain an investigator license.

## Earnings

Earnings of investigators, claims adjusters, and examiners vary significantly. Median annual earnings were $43,020 in 2002. The middle 50 percent earned between $33,120 and $56,170. The lowest 10 percent earned less than $26,680, and the highest 10 percent earned more than $71,350.

# Arson Investigators

Fire investigators determine the origins and causes of fires. They collect evidence, interview witnesses, and prepare reports on fires in cases where the cause may be arson or criminal negligence. They often are called upon to testify in court.

Arson investigators arrive at the scene of a fire and try to determine how it started. Although there are many types of fires, anything from a trash basket fire to a devastating forest fire, they all fall into just two categories: accidental or criminal.

Fire investigators check into both accidental and criminal fires. If there is an excessive monetary loss or a suspicion that the fire was not accidental, the arson investigator will conduct an in-depth check.

In the case of arson, the ultimate goal is not only to determine how the fire started, but also to find the arsonist. The work can be frustrating because evidence is often destroyed in the fire, making it difficult to catch and convict the criminal.

## Working Conditions

There are several dangers involved in arson investigation. Many building materials are made from plastic, which contains chemicals. Fumes escape when the temperature cools down after a fire, and arson investigators must wear masks with filters to protect their lungs from potentially toxic fumes. Shoveling through the debris in a burned-out building is also dangerous. A fire weakens all the structure's supports, and roofs can suddenly collapse, walls can cave in, and floors can give way.

Fire investigators sometimes have to work with the police or testify in court, so they need to have knowledge of the law and court procedure. They must have good writing skills, since the reports they write might be read in court. They must also have good speaking skills to provide convincing testimony.

## Training for Arson Investigators

Arson investigators must first complete regular firefighter training and serve their time as firefighters. Applicants for municipal fire-fighting jobs generally must pass a written exam; tests of strength, physical stamina, coordination, and agility; and a medical examination that includes drug screening. Workers may be monitored on a random basis for drug use after accepting employment.

Examinations are generally open to persons who are at least eighteen years of age and have a high school education or the equivalent. Those who receive the highest scores in all phases of testing have the best chances for appointment. The completion of community college courses in fire science may improve an applicant's chances for appointment. In recent years, an increasing proportion of entrants to this occupation have had some post-secondary education.

As a rule, entry-level workers in large fire departments train for several weeks at the department's training center or academy. Through classroom instruction and practical training, recruits study firefighting techniques, fire prevention, hazardous materials control, local building codes, and emergency medical procedures, including first aid and cardiopulmonary resuscitation. They also learn how to use axes, chain saws, fire extinguishers, ladders, and other firefighting and rescue equipment. After successfully completing this training, they are assigned to a fire company, where they undergo a period of probation.

A number of fire departments offer accredited apprenticeship programs lasting up to five years. These programs combine formal, technical instruction with on-the-job training under the supervision of experienced firefighters.

Technical instruction covers subjects such as firefighting techniques and equipment, chemical hazards associated with various combustible building materials, emergency medical procedures, and fire prevention and safety.

Fire departments often conduct training programs, and some firefighters attend training sessions sponsored by the National Fire Academy. These training sessions cover topics including executive development, anti-arson techniques, disaster preparedness, hazardous materials control, and public fire safety and education.

Some states also have extensive firefighter training and certification programs. In addition, a number of colleges and universities offer courses leading to two- or four-year degrees in fire engineering or fire science. Many fire departments offer firefighters incentives, such as tuition reimbursement or higher pay, for completing advanced training.

Most experienced firefighters continue studying to improve their job performance and prepare for promotion examinations.

To progress to higher-level positions, they acquire expertise in advanced firefighting equipment and techniques, building construction, emergency medical technology, writing, public speaking, management and budgeting procedures, and public relations.

Opportunities for promotion depend upon written examination results, job performance, interviews, and seniority. Increasingly, fire departments use assessment centers, which simulate a variety of actual job performance tasks, to screen for the best candidates for promotion.

The line of promotion usually is from firefighter to engineer, lieutenant, captain, battalion chief, assistant chief, deputy chief, and, finally, to chief. Many fire departments now require a bachelor's degree, preferably in fire science, public administration, or a related field, for promotion to positions higher than battalion chief. A master's degree is required for executive fire officer certification from the National Fire Academy and for state chief officer certification.

## Employment Figures

Paid career firefighters held about 282,000 jobs in 2002. First-line supervisors and managers of firefighting and prevention workers held about 63,000 jobs; fire inspectors held about 14,000.

About nine out of ten firefighting workers were employed by municipal or county fire departments. Some large cities employ thousands of career firefighters, while many small towns have only a few. Most of the remainder worked in fire departments on federal and state installations, including airports. Private firefighting companies employ a small number of firefighters and usually operate on a subscription basis.

In response to the expanding role of firefighters, some municipalities have combined fire prevention, public fire education, safety, and emergency medical services into a single organization commonly referred to as a public safety organization. Some local and regional fire departments are being consolidated into county-wide establishments in order to reduce administrative staffs and cut costs and to establish consistent training standards and work procedures.

## Job Outlook

Prospective firefighters are expected to face keen competition for available job openings. Many people are attracted to firefighting because it is challenging, provides the opportunity to perform an essential public service, requires only a high school education for entry, and guarantees a pension upon retirement after twenty years. Consequently, the number of qualified applicants in most areas exceeds the number of job openings, even though the written examination and physical requirements eliminate many applicants. This situation is expected to persist in coming years.

Employment of firefighters is expected to grow about as fast as the average for all occupations through 2012 as fire departments continue to compete with other public safety providers for funding. Most job growth will occur as volunteer firefighting positions are converted to paid positions. In addition to job growth, openings are expected to result from the need to replace firefighters who retire, stop working for other reasons, or transfer to other occupations.

Layoffs of firefighters are uncommon. Fire protection is an essential service, and citizens are likely to exert considerable pressure on local officials to expand or at least preserve the level of fire protection. Even when budget cuts occur, local fire departments usually cut expenses by postponing equipment purchases or not hiring new firefighters rather than through staff reductions.

## Earnings

Median hourly earnings of firefighters were $17.42 in 2002. The middle 50 percent earned between $12.53 and $22.96. The lowest 10 percent earned less than $8.51, and the highest 10 percent earned more than $28.22. Median hourly earnings were $17.92 in local government, $15.96 in the federal government, and $13.58 in state government. Median annual earnings of first-line supervisors and managers of firefighting and prevention workers were $55,450 in 2002. The middle 50 percent earned between $43,920 and $68,480. The lowest 10 percent earned less than $34,190, and the highest 10 percent earned more than $84,730. First-line supervisors and managers of firefighting and prevention workers employed in local government earned about $56,390 a year.

Median annual earnings of fire inspectors were $44,250 in 2002. The middle 50 percent earned between $33,880 and $56,100. The lowest 10 percent earned less than $26,350, and the highest 10 percent earned more than $69,060. Fire inspectors and investigators employed in local government earned about $46,820 a year.

Firefighters who average more than a certain number of hours a week are required to be paid overtime. The hours threshold is determined by the department during the firefighter's work period, which ranges from seven to twenty-eight days. Firefighters often earn overtime for working extra shifts to maintain minimum staffing levels or for special emergencies.

Firefighters receive benefits that usually include medical and liability insurance, vacation and sick leave, and some paid holidays. Almost all fire departments provide protective clothing (helmets, boots, and coats) and breathing apparatus, and many also provide dress uniforms.

Firefighters are generally covered by pension plans, often providing retirement at half pay after twenty-five years of service or if disabled in the line of duty.

# What It's Really Like

## Joe Nickell, Undercover Investigator

More than twenty years ago, Joe Nickell began his career as a private investigator for a world-famous detective agency. He has since taken another track and is now a paranormal investigator. But he got his start doing surveillance, background checks, and some dicey undercover work.

While working for the detective agency, Joe was part of a team of investigators doing undercover work. He describes the job as one that required a certain amount of flexibility: "We would work in a company's warehouse—as a stock clerk, shipper/receiver, mail clerk, fork-lift driver—wherever they could slip us in. Our job was really to become aware of and infiltrate theft rings operating there. We'd set them up and bust them. The work was done privately and secretly. We'd assure the owners that we could get rid of the problem without the whole story coming out.

"If the story did come out, it would result in bad morale. The employees would not be happy that the bosses had sent spies in. So, the police would not be involved. The company would handle it themselves, fire the men, and hope to keep the thieves out.

"Plus, the detective agency would not want its men to have to go to court. Once you did, and you were identified, it would mean the end of your undercover career. The agency would want to be able to use us again and again, not just one time."

Joe's job also included surveillance work, where he staked out a location that was under investigation. Much of his time was also spent on the telephone, performing background and character checks.

"Unlike some of the guys who hated doing any of the office work, I would go looking for the general work whenever I was between undercover assignments."

**Investigating Insurance Fraud.** Joe Nickell also worked on insurance fraud cases. "I was assigned to do surveillance on someone who was claiming he had a back injury. We staked out his house and watched him work on his car, photographing every move. He was bending over, darting up the steps two at a time. We documented it all."

# Chris Goodwin, Investigator

Chris Goodwin works as an investigator and office manager in the small solo-practice law firm owned by his wife, attorney M. J. Goodwin (see Chapter 2).

One of Chris's primary duties is to serve papers. If someone is being sued or getting divorced, he or she must be served the legal papers in person. As Chris says, "It involves a lot of time running around and trying to track people down."

Chris's investigative work has taken him on many different cases. "I've done things like follow cheating hearts around, taking their photos (in public places only—no Peeping Tom stuff). I also interview potential clients or current clients. It depends on what the case is. If it's a drug case, for example, and your client is in jail, you want to hear his or her side of the story. You'll already know the law enforcement side.

"Also, I occasionally interview witnesses in battered spouse cases. Right now I'm trying to find folks who've seen a man hit his wife or have seen her bruises. The client usually provides names to us but is often mistaken about whether or not a person is a witness. Some clients think that if they tell a witness something, that person is a witness. But that's not the case. The person has to speak from personal observations. I also help the wives file restraining orders."

Chris says that there is no typical day in his line of work—some days are busy, and others are slow. "But I like the freedom my job gives me. I'm not stuck at a desk all day, and I don't do the same thing over and over. I have to be creative to solve problems."

**How Chris Goodwin Got Started.** Chris's decision to enter this profession was the result of a very personal incident. "I became interested in investigative work later in life. My home was burglarized several years ago. Nobody really seemed to want to do anything about it. That bothered me, so I decided to learn more about law enforcement. I had to learn slowly; I couldn't quit my full-time job. I was working in the production lab at a chemical company as the senior lab technician, and I also worked in juvenile probation for about two years."

Although Chris wanted to enter law enforcement, he and his wife decided that investigative work would be a better choice. He was hired by a private detective agency and received lots of on-the-job training. In addition, Chris attended seminars at the Criminal Justice Academy, where he learned search and seizure, the laws of arrest, and public speaking and courtroom presentations. He is also a certified firearms instructor.

**Advice from Chris Goodwin.** Chris has some advice for anyone interested in investigative work: "Get with a pro and learn the ropes. It can be dangerous, and you need to know what to expect. A background in criminal justice can be helpful. You'll need to know the rules of evidence in order to obtain information that can be used in court.

"If you don't know what you are doing, you will not be able to effectively represent or help a client and may, in fact, do damage to the client's case. Having no investigator is better than having a bad one."

## Bob Lemons, Arson Investigator

Bob Lemons is a fire investigator for the Boca Raton, Florida fire-and-rescue department. He is also the handler of Holly, his partner on the job, an accelerant-detection canine.

While Bob enjoyed his work as a firefighter, he found the investigative work more interesting: "I watched the investigators come in at a fire, and I asked a lot of questions: 'Why are you doing this? Why are you looking here? What are you looking for?' I was persistent. After your supervisors get to know you and see that it's not just idle curiosity, they help you along."

Bob's supervisors were aware of his interest in fire investigation. Soon after he read a magazine article about accelerant canines being used by fire investigators, Bob told his chief that he would like to pursue investigation and work with a trained dog. He asked to be sent to the Maine State Police Canine Academy in Portland for five weeks, with a dog, to learn how to investigate fires.

Holly was donated by a local family and trained to search for the residue of flammable liquids. Upon detection of a combustible substance, Holly signals Bob, and samples are collected and sent to a lab for examination. Holly has actually helped to catch arsonists, who sometimes linger after a fire to watch the fire department at work. Bob walks Holly through a crowd to see if she detects the scent of an accelerant on anyone nearby. The police can then arrest that person for suspected arson.

According to Bob Lemons, fire investigation is a good job that allows you to interact with many people. Bob works with local police, the state fire marshal, and federal agencies.

Bob does admit, though, that the work can be frustrating: "The rewards of this job really are few and far between. That's because you can know how a fire started, know that it was arson, but you can't prove it in a court of law. A lot of times, you learn that the insurance company had to pay the claim even though you know the owner did it. Only about 4 percent of arsonists ever get caught and convicted. You get frustrated, but inside you know you did the best job you could do. You did your part."

# CHAPTER NINE

# Correctional Officers

Correctional officers are responsible for overseeing individuals who have been arrested and are awaiting trial or who have been convicted of a crime and sentenced to serve time in a jail, reformatory, or penitentiary. They maintain security and inmate accountability to prevent escapes, disturbances, or assaults. Correctional officers do not have any law enforcement responsibilities outside the institution where they work.

Police and sheriffs' departments in county and municipal jails or precinct station houses employ many correctional officers, also known as detention officers. Most of the approximately thirty-three hundred jails in the United States are operated by county governments, with about three-quarters of all jails under the jurisdiction of an elected sheriff. Individuals in the jail population change constantly as some are released, some are convicted and transferred to prison, and new offenders are arrested and enter the system.

Correctional officers in the U.S. jail system admit and process more than eleven million people a year. When individuals are first arrested, the jail staff may not know their true identity or criminal record, and violent detainees may be placed in the general population. This is the most dangerous phase of the incarceration process for correctional officers.

Most correctional officers are employed in large jails or state and federal prisons, watching over the approximately one million offenders who are incarcerated at any given time. In addition to jails and prisons, a relatively small number of correctional officers oversee individuals being held by the U.S. Immigration and Naturalization Service before they are released or deported. They also work for correctional institutions that are run by private for-profit organizations.

While both jails and prisons can be dangerous places to work, prison populations tend to be more stable than jail populations. Correctional officers in prisons know the security and custodial requirements of the prisoners with whom they are dealing.

Regardless of the setting, correctional officers maintain order and enforce rules and regulations within the institution. To help ensure that inmates are orderly and obey rules, correctional officers monitor the activities and supervise the work assignments of inmates. Sometimes, it is necessary for officers to search inmates and their living quarters for contraband such as weapons or drugs, to settle disputes between inmates, and to enforce discipline. Correctional officers periodically inspect the facilities, checking cells and other areas of the institution for unsanitary conditions, contraband, fire hazards, and any evidence of infractions of the rules. In addition, they routinely inspect locks, window bars, grilles, doors, and gates for signs of tampering. Finally, officers inspect mail and visitors for prohibited items.

Correctional officers report orally and in writing on inmate conduct and on the quality and quantity of work done by inmates. Officers also report security breaches, disturbances, violations of rules, and any unusual occurrences. They usually keep a daily log or record of their activities. Correctional officers cannot show favoritism and must report any inmate who violates the rules. Should the situation arise, they help the responsible law enforcement authorities search for escaped inmates or investigate crimes committed within their institution.

In jail and prison facilities with direct-supervision cell blocks, officers work unarmed. They are equipped with communications devices so that they can summon help if necessary. These officers often work in a cell block alone, or sometimes with another officer, among the fifty to one hundred inmates who reside there. The officers enforce regulations primarily through their interpersonal communications skills and the use of progressive sanctions, such as loss of some privileges.

In the highest-security facilities where the most dangerous inmates are housed, correctional officers often monitor the activities of prisoners from a centralized control center with the aid of closed-circuit television cameras and a computer tracking system. In such an environment, the inmates may not see anyone but officers for days or weeks at a time and may leave their cells only for showers, solitary exercise time, or visitors.

Depending on the offender's security classification within the institution, correctional officers may have to restrain inmates in handcuffs and leg irons to safely escort them to and from cells and other areas to see authorized visitors. Officers also escort prisoners between the institution and courtrooms, medical facilities, and other destinations outside the institution.

## Working Conditions

Working in a correctional institution can be stressful and hazardous. Every year, a number of correctional officers are injured in confrontations with inmates.

Correctional officers may work indoors or outdoors. Some correctional institutions are well lighted, temperature controlled, and well ventilated, while others are old, overcrowded, hot, and noisy.

Most correctional officers usually work eight-hour days, five days a week, on rotating shifts. Prison and jail security must be provided around the clock, which often means that officers work all hours of the day and night, including weekends and holidays. In addition, officers may be required to work paid overtime.

# Training for Correctional Officers

Most institutions require correctional officers to be U.S. citizens at least eighteen to twenty-one years of age; have a high school education or its equivalent; demonstrate job stability, usually by accumulating two years of work experience; and have no felony convictions. Promotion prospects may be enhanced through obtaining a postsecondary education.

Correctional officers must be in good health. Candidates for employment are generally required to meet formal standards of physical fitness, eyesight, and hearing. In addition, many jurisdictions use standard tests to determine an applicant's suitability to working in a correctional environment. Good judgment and the ability to think and act quickly are indispensable. Applicants are typically screened for drug abuse, subject to background checks, and required to pass a written examination.

Federal, state, and some local departments of corrections provide training for correctional officers based on guidelines established by the American Correctional Association and the American Jail Association. Some states operate regional training academies that are available to local agencies. All states and local correctional agencies provide on-the-job training at the conclusion of formal instruction, including instruction in legal restrictions and interpersonal relations. Many systems also require firearms proficiency and self-defense skills.

Officer trainees typically receive several weeks or months of training in an actual job setting under the supervision of an experienced officer. However, specific entry requirements and on-the-job training vary widely from agency to agency. Academy trainees generally receive instruction on a number of subjects, including institutional policies, regulations, and operations, as well as custody and security procedures.

As a condition of employment, new federal correctional officers must undergo 200 hours of formal training within the first year of employment. They also must complete 120 hours of specialized training at the U.S. Federal Bureau of Prisons residential training center at Glynco, Georgia, within the first sixty days after appointment. Experienced officers receive annual in-service training to keep abreast of new developments and procedures.

Some correctional officers are members of prison tactical response teams, which are trained to respond to disturbances, riots, hostage situations, forced cell moves, and other potentially dangerous confrontations. Team members receive training and practice with weapons, chemical agents, forced entry methods, crisis management, and other tactics.

With education, experience, and training, qualified officers may advance to correctional sergeant. Correctional sergeants supervise correctional officers and usually are responsible for maintaining security and directing the activities of other officers during an assigned shift or in an assigned area. Ambitious and qualified correctional officers can be promoted to supervisory or administrative positions all the way up to warden. Officers sometimes transfer to related areas, such as probation officer, parole officer, or correctional treatment specialist.

## Job Outlook

Job opportunities for correctional officers are expected to be excellent. The need to replace correctional officers who transfer to other occupations, retire, or leave the labor force, coupled with rising employment demand, will generate thousands of job openings each year. In the past, some local and state corrections agencies have experienced difficulty in attracting and keeping qualified applicants, largely due to relatively low salaries and the concentration of jobs in rural locations. This situation is expected to continue.

Employment of correctional officers is expected to grow faster than the average for all occupations through 2012, as additional officers are hired to supervise and control a growing inmate population. The adoption of mandatory sentencing guidelines calling for longer sentences and reduced parole for inmates will continue to spur demand for correctional officers. Moreover, expansion and new construction of corrections facilities are expected to create many new jobs for correctional officers, although state and local government budgetary constraints could affect the rate at which new facilities are built and staffed. Some employment opportunities also will arise in the private sector as public authorities contract with private companies to provide and staff corrections facilities.

Layoffs of correctional officers are rare because of increasing offender populations. While officers are allowed to join bargaining units, they are not allowed to strike.

## Earnings

Median annual earnings of correctional officers and jailers were $32,670 in 2002. The middle 50 percent earned between $25,950 and $42,620. The lowest 10 percent earned less than $22,010, and the highest 10 percent earned more than $52,370.

Median annual earnings in the public sector were $40,900 in the federal government, $33,260 in state government, and $31,380 in local government.

In the management and public relations industry, where the relatively small number of officers employed by privately operated prisons are classified, median annual earnings were $21,390.

According to the Federal Bureau of Prisons, the starting salary for federal correctional officers was about $23,000 a year in 2003. Starting federal salaries were slightly higher in selected areas where prevailing local pay levels were higher.

Median annual earnings of first-line supervisors and managers of correctional officers were $44,940 in 2002. The middle 50 percent earned between $33,730 and $59,160. The lowest 10 percent earned less than $29,220, and the highest 10 percent earned more than $69,370. Median annual earnings were $43,240 in state government and $49,120 in local government.

In addition to typical benefits, correctional officers employed in the public sector usually are provided with uniforms or a clothing allowance to purchase their own uniforms. Civil service systems or merit boards cover officers employed by the federal government and most state governments. Their retirement coverage entitles them to retire at age fifty after twenty years of service or at any age with twenty-five years of service.

## What It's Really Like

### Kimberly Diehl, Jailer

Kimberly Diehl is a jailer with the Harris County Sheriff's Department in Houston, Texas. Kimberly is responsible for 150 of the jail's 12,000 inmates. She works the 6 A.M. to 2 P.M. shift.

On a typical day, Kimberly and her partner conduct a head count of the inmates in their section, or quadrant. They distribute inmates' mail and escort inmates who are scheduled for activities such as clinic visits, classes, court, attorney visits, or recreation.

Kimberly and her partner must also enter the cell blocks every thirty minutes to check on inmates. They must also intervene whenever there is a fight among the inmates.

Overall, Kimberly likes her job: "I like the pay, of course. But I also like the shift I work. It gives me all evening to spend with my kids. I work with a good crew of deputies and a great sergeant.

"I'm not too pleased with the lack of sick time. When I first hired on in 1990, we were given fifteen sick days to use throughout the year. If you didn't use the sick time, it rolled over to the next year. Thus, you could accumulate quite a bit of sick time. Now, we are given three sick hours every payday. So in order to get one day of sick time, it would take a month and half.

"But in spite of the problems, I've found over the years that I could make a difference with the inmates. Not a 180-degree turn-around, mind you. Some of these inmates still come to jail, get out, and then come right back in.

"There are some, though, who are booked into jail, and it's their first time being in any kind of trouble. I try to help them. I'll encourage them to get their GED, for example. The jail provides schooling for those who haven't finished high school, and there's an office-practices class and a sewing class. I also try to encourage the drug abusers to sign up for the drug-abuse program. It's a very helpful program, and there are several who have learned their shortcomings and changed tenfold.

"I see people from all walks of life come through the jail, and to this day I haven't discovered what possesses someone to commit a crime."

**How Kimberly Diehl Got Started.** Kimberly began working in law enforcement with the Harris County Sheriff's Department in 1990. She was originally attracted by the salary, which was twice what she made in her previous job at a bank.

Kimberly immediately entered a two-week training course that taught jail procedures and defensive skills. "We did some role-playing. One of the instructors played the part of an inmate and the other instructor a deputy. We covered a variety of scenarios, such as an inmate threatening to kill himself with a razor or a deputy being attacked while making an enter inside the cell block. What do you do? There are several right answers to these two scenarios, but the most important thing we were told was to think logically."

Following the training course, Kimberly and the other new employees attended a one-week program that led to certification by the Texas Commission on Law Enforcement Standards and Education (TCLESE). "This is a tough week, which not only includes eight-hour-a-day class sessions, but also one day devoted to fire school. On this day we are required to put on an air mask and go through a smoke-filled building and search for possible inmates. Upon completion of the week, we are required to take the TCLESE test and, of course, we must pass it to continue working. If we don't, we go back through the program again."

**Advice from Kimberly Diehl.** Kimberly Diehl has some suggestions for anyone interested in working as a correctional officer: "My advice for anyone who pursues a career in law enforcement is to make sure you have the right mentality. Also, because the job is so stressful, one needs an 'out,' such as playing tennis, fishing, or just taking a long walk in the evening. One more thing—you must be in good physical shape. It is most assured you will get into a tussle on this job."

# CHAPTER TEN

# Security Guards

Guards, who are also called security officers, patrol and inspect property to protect against fire, theft, vandalism, terrorism, and illegal activity. These workers protect their employers' investments, enforce laws on the property, and deter criminal activity or other potential problems. They use radio and telephone communications to call for assistance from police, fire, or emergency medical services as the situation dictates. Security guards write comprehensive reports outlining their observations and activities during their assigned shifts. They may also interview witnesses or victims, prepare case reports, and testify in court.

Although all security guards perform many of the same duties, specific duties can vary based on whether the guard works in a "static" security position or on a mobile patrol. Guards assigned to static positions usually serve the client at one location for a specific length of time. These guards must become closely acquainted with the property and the people associated with it. They often monitor alarms and closed-circuit TV cameras.

In contrast, guards assigned to mobile-patrol duty drive or walk from location to location and conduct security checks within an assigned geographical zone. They may detain or arrest criminal violators, answer service calls concerning criminal activity or problems, and issue traffic-violation warnings.

Specific job responsibilities also vary with the size, type, and location of the employer. In department stores, guards protect people, records, merchandise, money, and equipment. They often work with undercover store detectives to prevent theft by customers or store employees, and they help in the apprehension of shoplifting suspects prior to arrival by police. Some shopping centers and theaters employ officers mounted on horses or bicycles who patrol the parking lots to deter car theft and robberies.

In office buildings, banks, and hospitals, guards maintain order and protect the institutions' property, staff, and customers.

At air, sea, and rail terminals and other transportation facilities, guards protect people, freight, property, and equipment. They may screen passengers and visitors for weapons and explosives using metal detectors and high-tech equipment, ensure nothing is stolen while being loaded or unloaded, and watch for fires and criminals.

Guards who work in public buildings such as museums or art galleries protect paintings and exhibits by inspecting people and packages entering and leaving the building.

In factories, laboratories, government buildings, data processing centers, and military bases, security officers protect information, products, computer codes, and defense secrets and check the credentials of all vehicles and people entering and leaving the premises.

Guards working at universities, parks, and sports stadiums perform crowd control, supervise parking and seating, and direct traffic. Security guards stationed at the entrance to places of adult entertainment, such as bars and nightclubs, prevent access by minors, collect cover charges at the door, maintain order among customers, and protect property and patrons.

Armored car guards protect money and valuables during transit. In addition, they protect individuals responsible for making commercial bank deposits from theft or bodily injury. When the armored car arrives at the door of a business, an armed guard enters, signs for the money, and returns to the truck with the valuables in hand. Carrying money between the truck and the business can be extremely hazardous for guards. Because of this risk, armored car guards usually wear bullet-proof vests.

All security officers must show good judgment and common sense, follow directions from supervisors, accurately testify in court, and follow company policy and guidelines. Guards should have a professional appearance and attitude and be able to interact with the public. They also must be able to take charge and direct others in emergencies or other dangerous incidents. In a large organization, the security manager is often in charge of a trained guard force divided into shifts, whereas in a small organization, a single worker may be responsible for all security.

Gaming surveillance officers and gaming investigators act as security agents for casino managers and patrons. They observe casino operations for irregular activities, such as cheating or theft, by either employees or patrons. To do this, surveillance officers and investigators often monitor activities from a catwalk over one-way mirrors located above the casino floor. Many casinos use audio and video equipment, allowing surveillance officers and investigators to observe these same areas via monitors. Recordings are kept as a record and are sometimes used as evidence against alleged criminals in police investigations.

## Working Conditions

Most security guards spend considerable time on their feet, either assigned to a specific post or patrolling buildings and grounds. Guards may be stationed at a guard desk inside a building to monitor electronic security and surveillance devices or to check the credentials of persons entering or leaving the premises. They also may be stationed at a guardhouse outside the entrance to a gated facility or community and use a portable radio or cellular telephone that allows them to be in constant contact with a central station.

The work usually is routine, but guards must be constantly alert for threats to themselves and the property they are protecting. Guards who work during the day may have a great deal of contact with other employees and members of the public. Gaming surveillance often takes place behind a bank of monitors controlling several cameras in a casino, which can cause eyestrain.

Guards usually work at least eight-hour shifts for forty hours per week and often are on call in case an emergency arises. Some employers have three shifts, and guards rotate to equally divide daytime, weekend, and holiday work. Guards usually eat on the job instead of taking a regular break away from the site. More than one in seven guards work part-time, and many individuals hold a second job as a guard to supplement their primary earnings.

## Training for Security Guards

Most states require that guards be licensed. To be licensed as a guard, individuals must usually be at least eighteen years old, pass a background check, and complete classroom training in such subjects as property rights, emergency procedures, and detention of suspected criminals. Drug testing often is required and may be random and ongoing.

Many employers of unarmed security guards do not have specific educational requirements. For armed guards, employers usually prefer individuals who are high school graduates or hold an equivalent certification. Many jobs require a driver's license. For positions as armed guards, employers often seek people who have had responsible experience in other occupations.

Guards who carry weapons must be licensed by the appropriate government authority, and some receive further certification as special police officers, which allows them to make limited types of arrests while on duty. Armed guard positions require more stringent background checks and entry requirements than those of unarmed guards because of greater insurance liability risks. Compared to unarmed security guards, armed guards and special police typically enjoy higher earnings and benefits, greater job security, and more advancement potential. They are usually given more training and responsibility.

Rigorous hiring and screening programs consisting of background, criminal record, and fingerprint checks are becoming the norm in the occupation. Applicants are expected to be in good health and have good character references and no serious police record. They should be mentally alert, emotionally stable, and physically fit in order to cope with emergencies. Guards in frequent contact with the public should be able to communicate well.

The amount of training guards receive varies. Training requirements are higher for armed guards because their employers are legally responsible for any use of force. Armed guards receive formal training in areas such as weapons retention and laws covering the use of force.

Many employers give newly hired guards instruction before they start the job and also provide on-the-job training. An increasing number of states are making ongoing training a legal requirement for retention of certification. Guards may receive training in protection, public relations, report writing, crisis deterrence, and first aid, as well as specialized training relevant to their particular assignments.

Guards employed at establishments placing a heavy emphasis on security usually receive extensive formal training. For example, guards at nuclear power plants undergo several months of training before being placed on duty under close supervision. They are taught to use firearms, administer first aid, operate alarm systems and electronic security equipment, and spot and deal with security problems. Guards authorized to carry firearms may be periodically tested in their use.

Although guards in small companies may receive regular salary increases, advancement opportunities are often limited. Most large organizations use a military type of ranking that offers the possibility of advancement in position and salary. Some guards may advance to supervisor or security manager positions. Guards with management skills may open their own contract security guard agencies.

In addition to the keen observation skills required to perform their jobs, gaming surveillance officers and gaming investigators must have excellent verbal and writing skills in order to document violations or suspicious behavior. They also need to be physically fit and have quick reflexes because they sometimes must detain individuals until local law enforcement officials arrive.

Surveillance officers and investigators usually do not need a bachelor's degree, but some training beyond the high school level is required; previous security experience is a plus. Several educational institutions offer certification programs. Training classes usually are conducted in a casino-like atmosphere using surveillance camera equipment.

## Job Outlook

Opportunities for security guards and gaming surveillance officers should be favorable in the future. Numerous job openings will stem from employment growth attributable to the desire for increased security and from the need to replace those who leave this large occupation each year.

In addition to full-time job opportunities, the limited training requirements and flexible hours attract many persons seeking part-time or second jobs. However, keen competition is expected for higher-paying jobs that require more training. These positions are usually found at facilities that require a high level of security, such as nuclear power plants or weapons installations.

Employment of security guards and gaming surveillance officers is expected to grow faster than the average for all occupations through 2012 as concern about crime, vandalism, and terrorism continue to increase the need for security. Demand for guards also will grow as private security firms increasingly perform duties, such as monitoring crowds at airports and providing security in courts, that were formerly handled by government police officers and marshals. Because enlisting the services of a security guard firm is easier and less costly than assuming direct responsibility for hiring, training, and managing a security guard force, job growth is expected to be concentrated among contract agencies.

Casinos will continue to hire surveillance officers as more states legalize gambling and as the number of casinos increases in states where gambling is already legal. Additionally, casino security forces will employ more technically trained personnel as technology becomes increasingly important in thwarting casino cheating and theft.

## Earnings

Median annual earnings of security guards were $19,140 in 2002. The middle 50 percent earned between $15,910 and $23,920. The lowest 10 percent earned less than $13,740, and the highest 10 percent earned more than $31,540.

Median annual earnings in the industries employing the largest numbers of security guards in 2002 were as follows:

| | |
|---|---|
| Elementary and secondary schools | $24,470 |
| General medical and surgical hospitals | $24,050 |
| Local government | $22,120 |
| Traveler accommodation | $21,390 |
| Investigation and security services | $17,910 |

Gaming surveillance officers and gaming investigators had median annual earnings of $23,110 in 2002. The middle 50 percent earned between $19,620 and $28,420. The lowest 10 percent earned less than $15,930, and the highest 10 percent earned more than $35,170.

## What It's Really Like

### Timothy T. Speed Jr., Security Supervisor

Timothy Speed is the security supervisor for a large apartment complex in Oklahoma City, Oklahoma. He has worked in this field since 1994.

The complex where Timothy works is usually considered a one-officer post, which is a location that requires only one officer for security. On weekends, however, the post often has up to three security officers on duty.

As Timothy describes it, "The atmosphere is mostly quiet on one-officer posts. Most days are a bit on the boring side. There are many times when you do nothing more than sit, stand, or patrol your post, and nothing happens. Then there are days you are so busy you wonder where the time went."

Timothy reports that working as a security officer at an apartment complex can be stressful because of the need to keep the peace among tenants. The security staff handles complaints about noise and domestic disturbances. As Timothy says, "These types of calls seem to build, with everything being quiet for months at a time, and then the tension breaks and everything goes wild.

"There are times that it can be very dangerous. Some people, who are not the most law-abiding to begin with, think that we security officers don't have the right to tell them what to do. Some of them would just as soon kill you as look at you.

"But really, most of the people are nice. The up side is that you get to meet a lot of people from all walks of life."

Timothy talks about the financial realities of his security job: "The downside to this work is that there is very little upward momentum. . . . With most security agencies I have worked for, I was lucky to get minimum wage.

"Here on this job, though, if I work full-time, I get a salary and an apartment. Part-time officers work thirteen hours a week in exchange for an apartment. All officers are required to live on the property in case something big happens."

**How Timothy Speed Got Started.** Timothy's interest in security work was a direct result of his desire to help others. As he describes it: "I wanted to do something to help people, and what better way to help people than to make them feel safe in their own homes and office buildings?

"The first security job I got was through a friend of mine whom I met at the local gun range. She was leaving a position with a security agency to start a job as a corrections officer. I applied and got the job, with my friend's recommendation, of course."

Timothy explains that in Oklahoma, all security officers must complete a training program to be fully licensed. Once he had a conditional license, Timothy attended training for an unarmed license. The program is forty hours long, and successful completion requires perfect attendance and a score of at least 80 percent on six tests.

Timothy has also had training for certification with an ASP baton, an expandable night stick. He has also been trained for licensure as an armed security officer. In addition, he has completed training to carry both a semiautomatic pistol and a twelve-gauge pump shotgun.

**Advice from Timothy Speed.** Timothy offers some realistic advice to aspiring security officers: "Firstly, my advice to anyone entering this field is to use the experience as nothing more than a stepping-stone to bigger and better things. A career as a police officer would be a good place to take this.

"In this field as a security officer, you sometimes will be placed in situations that not even some police officers would want to find themselves. And this provides practical experience for any law enforcement position.

"Secondly, always treat the people you will deal with the way you would want to be treated, but also keep them at a distance—because no human being is predictable. In essence, I am saying to treat every person as a possible threat.

"Lastly, if you can help it, never work an unarmed post because the firearm at your side is a great deterrent to would-be criminals. As a safety precaution, I suggest you purchase a bulletproof vest and wear it at all times while on duty.

"Always be alert, even if it's been quiet for months, because this is when things start to happen. Always, no matter what the person you are dealing with calls you, keep a professional attitude and perspective on the job. If you let them get to you, you have most definitely lost the battle and let them win.

"And you should realize that most security positions are worked at night, forty hours a week, including weekends, so if you're in this field, be prepared to give up weekends because that is when our job is done."

# Professional Associations

For additional information on the careers covered throughout this book, contact the appropriate professional associations listed below.

## Attorneys and Judges

The American Bar Association (ABA) provides information about the 188 ABA-approved law schools, bar admissions requirements, and other information on legal education.

American Bar Association
321 North Clark Street
Chicago, IL 60610
www.abanet.org

For educational and career opportunities for attorneys and judges in Canada, contact:

Canadian Bar Association
500–865 Carling Avenue
Ottawa, ON K1S 5S8
Canada
www.cba.org

Federation of Law Societies of Canada
445 Boulevard Saint-Laurent, Suite 480
Montreal, QC H2Y 2Y7
Canada
www.flsc.ca

Information on the LSAT, the Law School Data Assembly Service, applying to law school, financial aid for law students, and law schools in the U.S. and Canada may be found online through:

Law School Admission Council
www.lsac.org

# Court Staff

The professional association for clerks of the court is the National Conference of Appellate Court Clerks, which can provide you with career information as well as information about U.S. courts, both trial and appellate.

National Conference of Appellate Court Clerks
National Center for State Courts
300 Newport Avenue
Williamsburg, VA 23185
http://ncacc.ncsconline.org

For information about shorthand reporting, contact:

National Court Reporters Association
8224 Old Courthouse Road
Vienna, VA 22182
www.ncraonline.com

To learn of job openings for bailiffs, contact the clerk of the court or the chief bailiff in your jurisdiction.

..........................

# Paralegals

General information on a career as a paralegal and a list of paralegal training programs approved by the American Bar Association may be purchased from:

Division for Legal Services
American Bar Association
321 North Clark Street
Chicago, IL 60610
www.abanet.org/legalservices/legalassistants

For information on paralegal certification, training programs in specific states, and standards and guidelines, contact:

National Association of Legal Assistants
1516 South Boston, Suite 200
Tulsa, OK 74119
www.nala.org

For information on a career as a paralegal in Canada, contact the following:

Canadian Association of Paralegals
Postal box 967
Station B
Montreal, QC H3B 3K5
Canada
www.caplegal.ca

# Legal Secretaries

Persons interested in careers as legal secretaries can request information from:

National Association of Legal Secretaries (International)
314 East Third Street, Suite 210
Tulsa, OK 74120
www.nals.org

For information about continuing education, certification, and legal secretary careers, contact:

Legal Secretaries International
8902 Sunnywood Drive
Houston, TX 77088
www.legalsecretaries.org

# Law Enforcement Officers

Information about entrance requirements for police work may be obtained from federal, state, and local civil service commissions or police departments. For general police work information, contact:

International Union of Police Associations
1421 Prince Street, Suite 400
Alexandria, VA 22314
www.iupa.org

Links to all U.S. federal agencies are available at the White House website. Select the link for Agencies and Commissions:

www.whitehouse.gov/government

For information about Canadian law enforcement and federal agencies, contact:

Department of Justice Canada
284 Wellington Street
Ottawa, ON K1A 0H8
Canada
www.canada.justice.gc.ca

Canadian Security Intelligence Service
PO Box 9732
Postal Station T
Ottawa, ON K1G 4G4
Canada
www.csis-scrs.gc.ca

Customs and Revenue Agency
555 MacKenzie Avenue, Fourth Floor
Ottawa, ON K1A 0L5
Canada
www.cra-arc.gc.ca

Royal Canadian Mounted Police
RCMP Headquarters
1200 Vanier Parkway
Ottawa, ON K1A 0R2
Canada
www.rcmp-grc.gc.ca

# Investigators

For information on a career as a private detective or investigator, contact:

International Security and Detective Alliance
PO Box 6303
Corpus Christi, TX 78466

For information about insurance investigation, contact:

Insurance Institute of Canada
18 King Street East, Sixth Floor
Toronto, ON M5C 1C4
Canada
www.iic-iac.org

National Society of Professional Insurance Investigators
PO Box 88
Delaware, OH 43015
www.nspii.com

Contact the following organizations for information about careers in fire investigation:

International Association of Arson Investigators
12770 Boenker Road
Bridgeton, MO 63044
www.firearson.com

National Association of Fire Investigators
857 Tallevast Road
Sarasota, FL 34243
www.nafi.org

Canadian Association of Fire Investigators
One Crimson Ridge Road
Barrie, ON L4N 8P2
Canada
www.cafi.ca

# Correctional Officers

Information about entrance requirements, training, and career opportunities for correctional officers may be obtained from the Office of Personnel Management, the Federal Bureau of Prisons, state civil service commissions, state departments of correction, or nearby correctional institutions and facilities.

Information on professional development, accreditation, and careers is available from:

American Correctional Association
4380 Forbes Boulevard
Lanham, MD 10706
www.aca.org

# Security Guards

Further information about work opportunities for guards is available from local employers and the nearest state employment services office. Information about registration and licensing requirements for guards may be obtained from the state licensing commission or the state police department. In states where local jurisdictions establish licensing requirements, contact a local government authority such as the sheriff, county executive, or city manager.

# About the Author

A full-time writer of career books, Blythe Camenson works hard to help job seekers make educated choices. She firmly believes that with enough information, readers can find long-term, satisfying careers. Toward that end, she researches traditional as well as unusual occupations, talking to a variety of professionals about what their jobs are really like. In all of her books, she includes firsthand accounts from people who can reveal what to expect in each occupation.

Camenson was educated in Boston, earning her B.A. in English and psychology from the University of Massachusetts and her M.Ed. in counseling from Northeastern University.

In addition to *Careers for Legal Eagles*, she has written more than two dozen books for McGraw-Hill.